P9-CDE-782

Twayne's English Authors Series

Sylvia E. Bowman, *Editor*

INDIANA UNIVERSITY

Sir Philip Sidney

 114

Sir Philip Sidney

By ROBERT KIMBROUGH

University of Wisconsin

Twayne Publishers, Inc. :: New York

For

Lucy Johnston Ambler

Library of Congress Catalog Card Number: 71-120528

MANUFACTURED IN THE UNITED STATES OF AMERICA

Preface

The life and literary career of Sir Philip Sidney resemble those of John F. Kennedy and John Keats. Like the late President Kennedy, Sidney was an ambitious, dedicated, and philosophically oriented public servant whose sudden death in mid-life shocked the Western world into a self-conscious moment of honest reflection. His work, like Keats's, is marked by such amazing signs of growth and development that we are left wondering what possible achievements died with him. Differences, of course, abound— Kennedy, as President of the United States, was not merely a symbol of public life; and Keats was solely a poet. Still, the comparisons go far in suggesting both the impact of Sidney on his age and the far-reaching experimental nature of his art.

As is not the case with most Renaissance writers, the life of Sidney and the nature of his art must be studied together. The man is apparent everywhere in his works, although not the man of most popular accounts. To be sure, Sidney was for the Elizabethans, as he is for us, the image of the courtier par excellence; but the serious training and tough dedication needed to be a courtier in Elizabeth's day are often forgotten by us because of almost two centuries of generally romantic response to the ideal of courtly service, be it the influence of Sir Walter Scott, John Ruskin, or the cinema. To serve the Queen, however, was a hard, difficult, frustrating way of life, as Sidney was well aware from early youth; nevertheless, it was one that he had no choice in following. From the beginning, his was the education of a courtier; but that he should also be a writer involved neither complication nor contradiction. Both pursuits were encouraged by the educational program of "Art, Imitation, and Exercise," to use Sidney's casual phrase from the *Defence* (III, 37).

For a life to be whole or a poem fine, each of the three elements of this program had to be developed, but all had to be kept in balance. "Art" had to do with the personal skills and abilities needed to live or write, but these skills and abilities constantly increased in scope through learning the rules of conduct needed either to court a lady or to pen an epigram. "Imitation" was a call to follow the leadership of the great men and writers, past as well as present, either in the ways they had lived or written, or in what they had achieved in life or art. And "Exercise" meant practice, in school and out—the maintenance of an active intercourse with all of a man's worlds: academic, athletic, familial, social, courtly, literary, historical, national, religious, and international. As an esthetic theory, "Art, Imitation, and Exercise" led to a literary art that was learned, formal, and vital.

The doctrine of "Art, Imitation, and Exercise" was not entirely new with Sidney; it was the natural outgrowth of the Humanist movement in England which placed particular emphasis on the development of the whole man. What *is* new with Sidney is the way in which he sublimated this emphasis within his art in order to create works with their own hallmark: the "voice" of Sidney that is not biographically his, but esthetically so. This voice can be heard in *The Lady of May,* but it reaches maturity in *Astrophel and Stella.*

This mark of individuality in Sidney's art—his artistic integrity —is, then, directly related to the general Renaissance ethos of England. Indeed, a major purpose of this present study is to show Sidney's development within native traditions, for the tendency of other Sidney studies has been to emphasize his debts to Continental sources and influences. Real as these were, his major debts were English; and his achievements in fiction, criticism, and poetry are best understood within English contexts.

Although the theme of Sidney's artistic development within English tradition carries throughout, the book is organized by topic and general chronology: the life, the criticism, the early fiction, the poetry, and the late fiction. In the first chapter, there is no attempt to tell the whole story of Sidney's life; instead, a brief discussion of the five major periods is presented in order to see how they shaped the artist and affected the canon. Successive chapters are dedicated to the close study of the individual works of Sidney. A study of the *Defence* reveals his esthetic, one which can be seen as developing in *The Lady of May,* the *Old*

Arcadia, and the early poetry; as reaching maturity in *Astrophel and Stella;* and, finally, as being cast aside in Book III of the *New Arcadia.*

In undertaking a study of such scope in a book limited in length, I was immediately confronted with the problems of "audience" and "detail." The first problem was rather easily solved: I simply have assumed that any reader will most likely be one who is at least generally acquainted with English literature and the nature of Sidney's achievement. As for detail, I have tried not to rehash in the text points well covered by others; yet, at the same time, I have kept the notes few in number and short in length. In compensation, I have included a full and fully annotated bibliography of works which complement and supplement my study; and, when general reference is made to any of those works in the text, I have not burdened the reader with a needless note.

In Chapters 4 and 5, on the poetry, I have quoted from *The Poems of Sir Philip Sidney,* with the kind permission of the editor and the publisher, William Ringler and the Clarendon Press, Oxford, respectively. My debt to Mr. Ringler is much greater, however, than simple acknowledgment of, and thanks for, the fine texts which he has provided; for, because of the thoroughness of his introduction, the completeness of his presentation of background material, and the general soundness of his annotations a good deal more is known about Sidney's works than before. Although I do not agree with Mr. Ringler on every point—I do not accept his spelling "Astrophil," for example—the fact that the phrase "as Ringler has suggested" appears repeatedly in one form or another throughout this study shows the extent of my debt. Furthermore, I use his abbreviations on the assumption that they will be standard ones of the future.

In the chapters dealing with the prose I have used, again with permission, the original Feuillerat reissued in four volumes by the Cambridge University Press in 1962 as *The Prose of Sir Philip Sidney.* Although these volumes are not entirely reliable, they are now the only ones readily available; furthermore, although they do not represent authoritative texts, I have retained at the request of the editor of this series the original spelling and punctuation. Exceptions are cases of obsolete contractions and garbled meanings, where silent expansions and acknowledged corrections in punctuation have been made.

In Chapter 3, I have drawn in part from an article which appeared in *Renaissance Drama; New Series I* (1968), and in the Prologue and in Chapter 6 I have included some material from a paper which I read before the "Period of Spenser" section at the Modern Language Association meeting in December, 1965. The manuscript was completed during a part of a year spent at the Institute for Research in the Humanities, in Madison. I wish to thank the permanent members for their invitation, and the whole membership of 1965–66 for providing the atmosphere which made writing, reading, and research even more satisfying. For excellent typing, from first rough draft through final form, I wish to thank the patient ladies of the University of Wisconsin Department of English, especially Judith Merten Sowa and Sandra Gerstl Lesperance.

University of Wisconsin
Madison

ROBERT KIMBROUGH

Contents

Contents

Chronology

1554   Philip Sidney born, November 30, at Penshurst, Kent.
1557   Tottel's *Songes and Sonettes* first published.
1559   *A Mirror for Magistrates* first published.
1564   September, Sidney entered Shrewsbury Grammar School (Shropshire).
1566   Visited Oxford, where the Earl of Leicester, Sidney's uncle, entertained Queen Elizabeth I for a week.
1568   February (?), entered Corpus Christi College, Oxford; stayed three years.
1572   June to September, in Paris with Sir Francis Walsingham; witnessed St. Bartholomew's Day Massacre, August 24. September to June 1573, at Frankfort with Hubert Languet.
1573   Summer and early fall, en route to Italy via Heidelberg, Strasbourg, Hungary, and Vienna.
1573   November to October, 1574, lived in Venice and Padua; visited Florence and Genoa.
1574   Winter, at the Imperial Court in Vienna with Languet and Edward Wotton.
1575   Spring, returned home by way of Poland; arrived in England the first of June; July, at Kenilworth when Leicester entertained Queen Elizabeth I; August, saw father off to Ireland; fall and winter, at court.
1576   Made cupbearer to the Queen; sought out by Thomas Drant; Richard Edwards' *Paradise of Dainty Devices* first published. Summer, went to Ireland with Essex, and campaigned in the field with his father. November, returned to England with Essex's body; in December, embassy to Germany.
1577   February to June, with Fulke Greville and (later) Edward

Dyer, visited Thomas Wilson in Brussels, Don John of Austria in Louvain, Prince Casimir of the Palatinate in Heidelberg, Emperor Rudolf and Edmund Campion in Prague, and William of Orange in Holland. Spring, sister Mary married the Earl of Pembroke; Phillippe du Plessis Mornay arrived for a stay of a year and a half to plead in behalf of the Protestant cause. Summer and fall, active in behalf of Orange, the Netherlands, and "the cause"; defended in writing his father's conduct of Irish affairs. Christmas, at Wilton with his sister, and uncles Leicester and Warwick.

1578   January, exchanged gifts with the Queen. February, Sir Henry recalled from Ireland (returned to England in September). May, *Lady of May* presented during Queen's visit to Leicester at Wanstead. Spring, denied permission to fight in the Netherlands. Drant died; Thomas Proctor's *Gorgeous Gallery of Gallant Inventions* published. Summer (?), began *Old Arcadia.* December, John Lyly's *Euphues* published.

1579   January, Prince Casimir of the Palatinate and Languet visited England for a month. July, Jehan de Simier, the envoy of the Duc d'Anjou, revealed Leicester's secret marriage to the Earl of Essex's widow. August, Anjou arrived; Sidney argued with and challenged the Earl of Oxford before the French party; Stephen Gosson dedicated the *School of Abuse* to Sidney. September, opposed Anjou in letter to the Queen. October, Edmund Spenser mentioned the "Areopagus" and, in December, published *The Shepheardes Calender,* dedicated to Sidney.

1580   January, exchanged New Year's gifts with the Queen; took part in a tournament. Spring and summer, at Wilton finished *Old Arcadia.* Summer, Gabriel Harvey-Spenser correspondence published; Spenser went to Ireland with the new Lord Deputy, Lord Grey. September, Languet admonished Sidney concerning his long retirement with friends. Fall, Lyly's *Euphues' England* and Anthony Munday's *Zelauto* published; began *The Defence of Poesie.*

1581   January, elected to Parliament; Penelope Devereux, Essex's daughter, presented at court. March, Parliament dissolved, but Sidney remained at court; Penelope Devereux engaged to Lord Rich (married him in November). May, the tournament of the "Fortress of Desire." Summer, having finished *The Defence* and most of the *Certaine Sonets* and his share of *The Psalms,* Sidney began *Astrophel and Stella.* September, Languet died; Phillippe du Plessis Mornay published *The Truth of Religion.* Fall, at court; Christmas, at Wilton.

1582   February, part of lavish escort for Anjou to the Netherlands. Late spring and summer in Wales with father; finished *Astrophel and Stella;* began the *New Arcadia.*

1583   January, knighted in order to be proxy for Prince Casimir at Knight of the Garter installation. March, Sir Henry Sidney's long letter to Sir Francis Walsingham concluded almost two years of negotiation for the marriage of Philip and Frances Walsingham (married in September). Spring, finally officially appointed as assistant to his uncle the Earl of Warwick, the Master of Ordinance. Suspended work on the *New Arcadia* and began translating Du Mornay's *Truth of Religion.*

1584   February, dinner at Fulke Greville's with Giordano Bruno, John Florio, and Matthew Gwinne. Fall, defended Leicester in writing. September, when about to go with Sir Francis Drake to America, finally appointed Governor of Flushing (arriving in November).

1586– Summer, father and mother died; September 22, wounded
1587   at Zutphen; October 17, died at Arnheim; February 16, 1587, buried with great ceremony in St. Paul's.

1590   *New Arcadia* published by William Ponsonby; Frances married Robert, Earl of Essex, son of Walter Devereux and brother of Penelope.

1591   *Astrophel and Stella* published twice by Thomas Newman and once by Matthew Lownes.

1593   *The Arcadia* (the *New Arcadia* "augmented and ended" by a slightly revised version of the last three books of the *Old Arcadia*) published by Ponsonby for the Countess of Pembroke.

1595   *The Defence of Poesie* published by Ponsonby and, as *An Apologie for Poetrie,* by Henry Olney.

1598   *The Countesse of Pembrokes Arcadia . . . with sundry new additions* (the "collected works") published by Ponsonby for the Countess of Pembroke. (Added *Certaine Sonets* and *The Lady of May,* retained the 1593 *Arcadia,* but did not print the *Old Arcadia.*)

1926 *Old Arcadia* first published by Feuillerat. (Since 1907, nine manuscripts of the whole work, prose and poetry, have been discovered, and one more of the poems alone.)

Prologue

ON nine ascending stages, the lords and ladies of her court are arranged in appropriate order; on a tenth, placed against a background of the sun and the signs of the crystalline sphere, the Lady of Perfect Beauty is herself enthroned. Suddenly in front of her castle, at the sounding of trumpets, four knights, richly caparisoned and handsomely attended, emerge from a high-framed siege castle built of earth. Their Herald of Arms, dressed in red and white, identifies the knights as the adopted sons of Lady Desire, who has nurtured them and raised them to believe that love of true Virtue can be maintained only by forceful activity. In that belief, and in the service of Desire, they come forth to challenge this fortress of Perfect Beauty and to demand the surrender of the high-minded Lady. Immediately Angels, Lords, and Everyman (represented by Adam and Eve) rush to her defense, unanimous in the belief that "Desire dooth not deserve one winke of good favour from Ladie Beautie's smiling eies, for threatning to win her fort by force."

After two days of exhausting individual and mass trials, the Four Foster Children of Desire are finally overcome and confess their folly: their Herald says, "They acknowledge the blindnesse of their error, in that they did not know Desire (how strong soever it be) within itself to be stronger without itself than it pleased the desired. They acknowledge they have degenerated from their fosterer in making Violence accompanie Desire. They acknowledge that Desire received his beginning and nourishment of this fortresse, and therefore to commit ungratefulnesse in bearing armes (though desirious armes) against it. They acknowledge noble Desire should have desired nothing so much, as the flourishing of that fortresse. . . . They acknowledge the least determination of Vertue (which stands for the gard of this fortresse) to be too strong for the strongest Desire; and therefore they doo acknowledge themselves overcome, as to be slaves to this Fortresse for ever, which title they will beare in their foreheads, as their other name is ingraven on their hearts."[1]

This description is not of an episode from the *New Arcadia,* but of a triumph staged at the Court of Queen Elizabeth in May, 1581, the "invention" of the Earl of Arundel, Baron Windsor of Stanwell, Fulke-Greville, and Philip Sidney. The word "invention" is that used by Henry Goldwell in his account of the triumph, and the term is sufficient to remind us of the unself-conscious merging in the sixteenth century of the disciplines of rhetoric, art, and life. The result of this merging is, paradoxically, a highly self-conscious literary art, but it explains why a triumph at court *is* like an episode in a heroic romance: both are imitations, that idea in rhetoric, art, and life based squarely on the principle of *inventio,* the manipulation and arrangement of things known. As a result, the quality of invention determines the quality of an imitation; for invention reveals the genius of the author, his cast and play of mind, his innate sensitivity—and determines whether his imitation is to be judged as merely conventional or as genuine.

The most obvious way a work of literature takes on an existence separate from the author is the way it can be identified as a member of a genre. The sixteenth-century tendency toward the neo-Classical criticism of literature, which was a natural outgrowth of the Medieval love of categories applied to the renaissant interest in ancient letters, was nurtured by the doctrine of imitation, which called for a traditional manner of treatment of new matter or the recasting of old matter by following the rules for a traditional form. As a result, Renaissance art is highly conventional and artificial. But this quality did not prevent genuineness or even greatness, for the integrity and energy of the artist are not necessarily compromised or repressed just because either his modes or his subjects are traditional. But the doctrine of imitation tends to restrict a person's view of life; and, if this implication becomes clear to an artist whose whole attention *is* life (or verisimilitude), the shock could be paralyzing, even were he a great artist.

CHAPTER 1

A Life of Art, Imitation, and Exercise

THE son of a Tudor nobleman got far more indoor schooling than did any of his predecessors; still, the major part of his education came from "exercise," from direct conversation with the world—and what a world! Surely the *angst* of our revolutionary atomic world is real; but it is indirect, it is learned, it is truly cultured; the influence of the revolutionary Tudor world on personality was direct. Gunpowder was too new to fear, but the new nation founded by Henry VII, and the new religion started by Martin Luther and tentatively established in England by Henry VIII in the 1530s, created an explosive enough atmosphere to make all noblemen wonder how long their worlds, large and small, would hold together.

Tudor materialism and love of ritual were sublimations of this anxiety, but the new learning of Thomas Linacre, William Grocyn, and Thomas More, John Cheke, Roger Ascham, and Thomas Wilson provided an approach to life capable of stabilizing and directing the emergent nationalism and Protestantism by making all men aware of their common heritage, shared nature, and collective destiny, as well as making each man aware of his inherent power, individual responsibility, and glorious potential. C. S. Lewis to the contrary, the Humanists' conception of "art" as skill, a technical proficiency which could be taught and developed through "imitation," was progressive at the same time that it was conservative. Sir Philip Sidney's life is a case in point.

I *1554–1572: Art*

The curious paradox of simultaneous turbulence and continuity, of chaos and calm, that marks sixteenth-century England can be seen in the details surrounding Philip Sidney's birth and baptism in 1554. He was born on November 30 at Penshurst, that famous thirteenth-century castle in Kent which to Ben Jonson symbolized the stability of England, but which in reality seemed to have changed hands with the accession of each new monarch since Henry III. In fact, only in 1552 had Sidney's grandfather, Sir William, received it from Edward VI. Sir William's son Henry had been the boyhood companion and adult counsellor of Protestant Edward and was the son-in-law of a recently executed rebel, the Earl of Northumberland; still, just before the birth of Philip, Henry had been sent by Catholic Queen Mary to escort to England her husband-to-be, the King of Spain. Philip's mother, the former Mary Dudley, had been ever since childhood the friend and companion of Princess Elizabeth; but she had helped her father, the Earl of Northumberland, in his plot to put his son Guilford and Lady Jane Grey on the throne in 1553. Philip's Dudley uncles, under Elizabeth to become the powerful Earls of Leicester and Warwick, who also had taken part in this Protestant plot, had just been released from prison by Mary. But all along, his Sidney aunts had been lifelong, devoutly Catholic companions of Queen Mary. The Sidneys were either naively daring or coolly diplomatic; for Philip's godparents, they picked the widowed Duchess of Northumberland and King Philip. The ultimate irony of this complex situation is that, as Philip Sidney grew up, Philip of Spain became more and more the target of his political and religious anger.

As M. W. Wallace, Sidney's most reliable biographer, observed, that Northumberland would consider Sir Henry as a proper husband for his daughter is proof enough that the Sidneys were considered one of the leading families of England in a time when "position" was more than a figurative expression. The Sidneys, like the Dudleys, were of the "new" England—Tudor England. Although both families had long been numbered among the respected gentry, not until the Wars of the Roses cut a swath through the peerage was their elevation possible; but the Dudleys rose higher and more quickly. Sir William Sidney had been made a Knight of the Garter by Henry VIII, and his son Henry was knighted by Edward. Still, though both received various small grants from their kings, held sundry crown offices, and undertook several missions of peace and war, by the time of the death of Edward, peerage had escaped them. With the coronation of Mary, a major step upward for the Sidneys appeared to be the appointment of Sir Henry as Governor General of Ireland in 1556, a position which put him second in command to the Lord Deputy, his stormy brother-in-law Fitzwalter, the future Earl of Sussex under Elizabeth. Sir Henry remained in Ireland under Elizabeth, even replacing Sussex as Lord Deputy; was appointed Lord President of Wales in 1560, a position which he held for life; and was enrolled in the Order of the Garter in 1564. But Sir Henry's sensible, fair, and conscientious conduct of Irish affairs cost him his health, wealth, and good favor at court. When finally, early in 1572, Elizabeth offered him a peerage, it was without grant of land or money; and Sir Henry was too poor, proud, and practical to accept.

Two other avenues of advancement seemed open to the Sidneys but they, too, were blocked off by the end of 1571. Lady Mary had nursed Queen Elizabeth throughout the most serious illness of her reign, the smallpox of 1562. Had the Queen died, civil war would have been inevitable, but Lady Mary's only reward was a total disfiguration from the disease, which the Queen was spared. Then, in 1568, and possibly earlier, William Cecil, Lord Burghley, Elizabeth's closest and most powerful councillor, began the subtle parry and thrust of negotiation with Sir Henry to arrange for a marriage between Philip and his daughter Anne. Burghley, as did all who met him even in his extreme youth, saw in Philip a youngster of promise. But it eventually became clear to Cecil that the Sidneys were losing their wealth and favor at court, and by the end of 1570 the negotiations were dormant; in 1571 Cecil blessed the sudden and unlooked-for proposal of the Earl of Oxford to marry Anne. There is much evidence that the nearly two years of negotiation between Burghley and Sir Henry were public knowledge, but there is no evidence whatsoever about what Anne and Philip may have felt for each other—if anything.

Although Philip's family fortunes were arrested by 1572, his own seemed bright indeed, especially because he could be considered the heir of Elizabeth's favorite, Robert Dudley, Earl of Leicester. Furthermore, he could thank his family for having provided him with a sound education, first at home in Kent until September, 1564; then at the grammar school of Shrewsbury in Wales; and finally at Oxford (and possibly Cambridge) for at least the three years 1568–71. His parents were themselves products of the new learning developed by the Humanists. Sir Henry, according to Anthony à Wood, attended Oxford; as companion to Prince

Edward, he must have conversed with Sir John Cheke and Roger Ascham; and, among his last efforts before being recalled as Lord Deputy of Ireland in 1571, was the founding of a number of grammar schools, in which he was successful, and of a university in Dublin, in which he was not.

Lady Mary Sidney, along with Elizabeth and Lady Jane Grey, was of the first generation of English ladies for whom tutors and formal education were provided. Thus, even though Lady Mary's husband was away on crown business during most of the first ten years of Philip's life, she was amply trained to oversee and even conduct his elementary education. In 1564, the grammar school at Shrewsbury was a logical choice, not merely because it was only thirty miles from Ludlow, the presidential seat of Wales, but mainly because, under the headmastership of Thomas Ashton, it was fast becoming one of the most respected preparatory schools for Oxford and Cambridge. At both Shrewsbury and Oxford (which remained less innovative than Cambridge) the curriculum was founded squarely upon the trivium: grammar, rhetoric, and logic. In both places, the main emphasis fell on rhetoric because it exploited grammar and employed logic.

Thanks mainly to Roger Ascham, we have a rather full picture of the nature and bias of Elizabethan education; and thanks to scholars such as T. W. Baldwin (*Shakspere's Small Latine and Lesse Greeke*), Virgil Whitaker (*Shakespeare's Use of Learning*), and Madeleine Doran (*Endeavors of Art*) we have a detailed knowledge of its content and regimen. Analysis of the works of Sidney (especially of *The Defence of Poesie*) supports their contention that the emphasis placed by the Humanists on rhetoric was not an end in itself; rhetoric, as Miss Doran has commented, "was one of the tools of that expressiveness that so informs Elizabethan life" (32). Furthermore, rhetoric was not a tool of limited uses; it was a means of amassing knowledge and of cultivating skill through an exposure to tradition and a utilization of individual talent in order to prepare one to cope with the world. It was, in short, the tool of "Art, Imitation, and Exercise." To shift the focus, the "3 R's" of Elizabethan education were: Reason, Rhetoric, and Religion. The first was assumed, for it defined man's unique nature: a rational animal. The last was the end, for it provided the context for comprehending all of life. The burden on

rhetoric, then, was immense: it was the means by which man culti-
vated his reason in order to prepare his soul for heaven.[1]

At both Shrewsbury and Oxford attendance at divine service
was mandatory and religion was tied in closely with the curriculum, most obviously so when Sunday's sermon would be the subject for analysis in Monday morning's rhetoric class. Even at
college, and especially at Oxford, public discourse and formal
disputation were central, influencing everything written and spoken,
from letters home to student plays. In fact, the visit of Elizabeth
to Oxford in 1566, then under the chancellorship of Leicester,
can best be understood as a series of rhetorical displays, each in a
properly prescribed form. Young Sidney was there, attended by
Thomas Wilson, author of *The Arte of Rhetorique* (1553).

Because Sidney in 1568 attended Oxford as the nephew of the
chancellor and as the son of the Lord Deputy of Ireland, we can
be sure that the handful of young men soon to distinguish themselves from the some fifteen hundred students registered in the
university knew, or knew of, Sidney. In addition to Fulke Greville,
who had been at Shrewsbury with him, there were: William Camden, to become England's first distinguished historian; Richard
Hakluyt, propagandist for Elizabethan exploration; Walter Raleigh,
his contemporary, but never a warm friend; Thomas Bodley, lifelong university man; John Lyly, whose *Euphues* was to appear
while Sidney was engaged in writing the *Old Arcadia;* Richard
Stanyhurst, translator of the *Aeneid* in hexameters; Richard
Hooker, the great apologist for the Elizabethan Settlement; and
Edmund Campion and Robert Parsons, friends of Sir Henry who
became recusant martyrs.

This enumeration is important in understanding the life and art
of Sidney because it provides a sound reminder of just how small
Elizabethan England was, and of how, with its structured society,
anyone who was anyone at all knew or could know everyone else.
If today we can still speak accurately of an Establishment, made
up of peers, civil servants, and the intelligentsia, all centered in
London, how much more accurately can the term be applied to
Elizabeth's day, when the London area at the time of her death
could not have had a population of much over two hundred
thousand. In fact, the details of Sidney's grand tour of 1572–75
prove that the international community of the day was itself quite
small.

II   *1572–1575: Exercise*

The "exercise" of the grand tour developed Sidney amazingly. He left, in the words of Leicester, "young and raw"; but a year after his return Elizabeth employed him on an important diplomatic mission. Part of the reason for this development can be attributed to the good luck of Sidney's falling into the hands of Hubert Languet, distinguished scholar (educated at Padua), fervent Protestant (converted by Melanchthon), and trusted diplomat (although French, the representative of the Elector of Saxony both at Paris and at the Imperial Court, first in Vienna and then in Prague, and a close consultant to the Prince of Orange). Because most of the extensive Sidney-Languet correspondence has long been readily accessible, the temptation to overemphasize the influence of this man, nearly forty years older than Sidney, is great. He probably did not change one iota the essential Sidney; but, as a kind of tutor in international affairs and tour guide, in person and in letters, he was a beneficial directing spirit. That Sidney respected Languet can be seen in his following his mentor's advice neither to visit that den of iniquity, Rome, nor to venture closer than Venice to the iron curtain separating the Turk from Europe. Moreover, when young Robert Sidney set out for Europe, his older brother's letters sound much like Languet's to him!

Sidney met Languet upon arriving in Paris at the court of Charles IX in June, 1572, when he stayed with Languet's friend, the English ambassador and his own future father-in-law, Sir Francis Walsingham. Charles was so taken by Sidney that he created him a baron, a clear indication of the manner in which Sidney was welcomed in the highest circles. Philip surely met as well the dowager Catherine de' Medici and her other Valois children: the Duke of Anjou, former suitor to Queen Elizabeth and soon to succeed his brother as Henry III; the Duke of Alençon, soon to succeed his brother as suitor and as Anjou; and Margaret, whose forced marriage to Henry of Navarre he witnessed on August 18. This marriage was intended to bring the same kind of peace to France that Henry Tudor's marriage to Anne, daughter of Edward IV, had brought to England; but it brought on instead the death of the Huguenot leader, Admiral de Coligny, and the resultant massacre on St. Bartholomew's Day. Before this fatal

event Sidney had met the most important Protestants: Admiral de
Coligny and his wife, soon to marry William the Silent, Prince of
Orange; Phillippe du Plessis Mornay, for whose daughter he would
be godfather in London in 1578 and whose *Truth of Religion*
(1581) he would begin but never finish translating; and Peter
Ramus, famous rhetorician whose anti-Aristotelian views seem
to have supplemented but did not supplant the bias of Sidney's
Shrewsbury-Oxford education. Whether or not he met the members of the Pléiade and De Baïf's Academy, as John Buxton
(whose account of the grand tour is full and suggestive) says, "he
certainly knew of their discussions and their poetry" (49), if only
from the firsthand testimony of Languet.

After the St. Bartholomew's Day Massacre, but before letters
from England came requesting Sidney's return home, Walsingham
decided that Sidney should leave Paris and sent him to Languet
and Andreas Wechel, the printer, who had fled to Frankfort.
There Sidney had the leisure to study firsthand the frictions and
nascent alliances among the emerging Protestant states within the
old Holy Roman Empire; but, of more present concern was the
chance the visit afforded to meet some of the famous Humanist
printers and scholars, most notably Henri Estienne (Henry Ste-
phens) in Heidelberg and Johan Sturm, friend of Ascham and
admired by Burghley, in Strasbourg. When Languet was soon re-
assigned to the court of Maximilian in Vienna, Sidney followed in
the late spring of 1573, arriving late in the summer. After a brief
stay he accompanied Languet's contemporary, the famous pioneering botanist, Charles de l'Ecluse, on an extended field trip into
Hungary; upon his return, he departed for Italy.

Then, as today, no matter what other countries are visited, Italy
had to be included if the grand tour was to be complete, but not
so much because of her antiquities. Italy was the center of all that
was new, fashionable, creative, and modern. For very different but
obvious reasons, Ascham and Burghley both advised against such
trips. But Sidney, brought up on the literature of ancient Italy and
born in a country which he had been taught to believe was barren
of letters, must have anxiously crossed "the craggie rocks of
th' Alpes" (in the words of his traveling companion Lodowick
Bryskett). In Italy, learned and native drama were flourishing,
Petrarch had showed that Italian could sing, Ariosto (not Dante)
had proved that man could attain the heroic even in the vernacu-

lar, the academies and presses were pouring forth the wisdom
of the ancients and the commentaries of the moderns, and the
arts were everywhere to be seen. In Venice, during Sidney's stay,
Palladio was designing, Palestrina composing, and Titian still paint-
ing. When Languet asked for a portrait, Sidney favored Veronese
over Tinteretto.

But of these experiences, no reactions of Sidney survive. We do
not even know whether he met Tasso during a short residence in
Padua, or whom he may have met in Florence. But from the
Languet correspondence we do know something of Sidney's study.
Besides satisfying his thirst for political, military, economic, and
geographical information (Machiavelli), we know he added fluency
in Italian to his mastery of French; learned some Spanish; began
to pursue Greek beyond rudimentary grammar in order to read
Aristotle, a favorite, and continued his study of Latin. Although
we know less of the year's stay than we would like, these few
details suggest a full exposure to the high Renaissance in Northern
Italy.

Sidney returned to Vienna in November, 1574, where, after a
trip to Poland, he spent the winter at the court. At this time, as
we are reminded by the delightful opening of *The Defence of
Poesie,* Sidney met Edward Wotton, who was to remain his close
friend. We have no letters giving details concerning his stay, for
he was with Languet; but his experience was such that Elizabeth
asked him to return as her personal representative in less than two
years when Maximilian died and was succeeded by his son Rudolph. In the spring of 1575, Sidney and Wotton began a leisurely
trip north, renewing previous acquaintances both political and
learned; and they finally arrived in England almost three years to
the day after Sidney's day of departure.

III *1575–1580: "The expectancy and rose of the fair state"*

The next five years were among the most exciting and frustrating of Sidney's life. As soon as he returned he was caught up in
the whirl of court life, accompanying the Queen on her stately
summer progress, the most notable entertainment in the course
of which was presented by Leicester at Kenilworth. While Sidney
was still on the Continent, the Queen had been prevailed upon
to reappoint Sir Henry as Lord Deputy in Ireland. No one else
had made such an honest effort to bring justice, even though a

peculiarly harsh Protestant English kind of justice, to Ireland with
no regard for personal gain. To Elizabeth, this effort simply meant
more direct expense to her. She was reluctant to return Sir Henry
for the simple reason that she knew he would try to do his job.
But Walter Devereux, Earl of Essex, had returned, confessing
failure in his miltary efforts to tame the Irish; and Sir Henry
reluctantly, but much to the joy of the Irish, undertook in August
his old post as Lord Deputy.

For the next year Philip Sidney was active at court, seeking
employment and taking part in festivities. His attractive presence
was rewarded in the spring of 1576 when the Queen made him
her cupbearer. During this time, Essex, who was at court trying
to refurbish his tarnished fortunes, real and political, was much
drawn to Sidney; and part of his plans for stabilizing his future
seems to have been the negotiation of a marriage between Philip
and his then eleven-year-old daughter Penelope. When Essex returned to Ireland in the summer now as head of the army only,
Sidney accompanied him in order to join his father who was cam-
paigning in the field. During August, Essex fell mortally ill in
Dublin, put his affairs in order, and sent for Philip, according to a
second-hand report, in order to urge the marriage contract. However, Essex died before he could return from the field, and Sidney
accompanied the body back to England in November and helped
with the funeral arrangements. Sir Henry, who had never been
fond of Essex, was not tempted by a deathbed plea to carry
through a contract which would only mean an additional drain
on his already meager wealth; and the marriage negotiations were
broken in November.

In December, the Queen called upon Philip to undertake the
kind of mission that he had been eager for ever since his return to
England: he was named head of an embassy to the Holy Roman
Empire to convey to Rudolph the Queen's sympathies for the
recent death of his father Maximilian and congratulations for his
election to the imperial throne. A similiar mission to the Palatinate
was incorporated, for the Elector had also recently died, being
replaced by his son Louis. Naturally, the real purpose of the embassy was to find out the new Emperor's inclinations with regard
to England specifically and to Protestantism in general. In this
later regard the trip to the Palatinate was especially important;
for Louis's brother Casimir was known to be a truly militant

Protestant. As proved by the Languet correspondence, Sidney was openly enthusiastic concerning the possibilities of a "Protestant League" that would be powerful enough to ignore France and to mount direct force against Spain (hence, the Empire). The initial point of attack would be the Low Countries now under the governorship of the fiery Spaniard, Don John of Austria, the hero in the battle against the Turks at Lepanto, whom Sidney had met previously in Vienna. Hence, Sidney was anxious to include a visit with William of Orange on his trip, but Languet wisely counseled against a move not expressly endorsed by the Queen. Fortunately, while Sidney was on his homeward progress Edward Dyer came bringing, with the Queen's permission, Leicester's request that Sidney stand in as godfather to William's new daughter.

There is no need to repeat in detail the personal success of Sidney in the various courts and great houses he visited. His magnetism was such that all who met him were won, and the metaphor that abounds is "shiny star of the English court." Proof of the high expectations people held for Sidney is the fact that William found him sufficiently attractive and promising to attempt to tie the Protestant hopes of the Low Countries, Holland and Zealand, to England through a marriage between Sidney and his sister. When we recall that even domestic marriages were consummated with the same care, investigation, and legal protraction that went into any other kind of financial merger, the importance of this international marriage is obvious. To the English, such a marriage could be second in importance only to one for Queen Elizabeth; and, so long as she was unmarried, she was not about to let any subject make an illustrious foreign alliance.

Although Sidney returned in personal triumph (or possibly *because* he did), the Queen gave him no official position in the court or council; not until the fall of 1585 did she call on him to undertake any crown business other than minor escort duty. Specifically, Sidney in his enthusiastic support of the Protestant "cause," seems to have implied to Casimir that Elizabeth was more interested in a Protestant league than she actually was; for she immediately sent an ambassador to counteract the implication. Sidney was a high-minded, quick-tempered activist—a combination of qualities entirely antithetic to the Queen's mode of operation. He was attractive enough to help swell a progress and clever enough to stage and take part in a tournament; but he was too

independent in his thinking, as can be seen in the 1579 challenge
to Oxford and in the letter to the Queen opposing the Anjou marriage, to be trusted with serious business. As a result of the
Queen's attitude, Sidney had time from the early fall of 1579 to
early fall of 1585 for more private matters and personal concerns.

IV   *1580–1585: Imitation*

During the summer and fall of his most public discontent,
Sidney became more and more the center for a circle of literary
friends, the most important of whom was Edmund Spenser. The
immediate and most conspicuous product of this group was *The
Shepheardes Calender,* published in December and dedicated to
Sidney; but Sidney had already written *The Lady of May* and was
at work on the five books and four eclogues of the *Old Arcadia,*
which he finished in 1580. The conversation with friends and work
on the *Old Arcadia* led Sidney into the more serious considerations of art which resulted in *The Defence of Poesie* (written
1580–82). These considerations, together with his past experiments in prosody (the eclogues and *The Psalms,* written before
1580), led to a brief but studied flirtation with quantitative English verse before he settled securely in accentual syllabic verse for
most of the *Certaine Sonets* and for *Astrophel and Stella* (written
1581–82). After completing the *Defence* and *Astrophel,* Sidney
resumed the writing of prose fiction, revising the *Old Arcadia* so
drastically that the nearly completed three books which he put
aside in 1583 must be called the *New Arcadia* (although scholars
and critics, aware of the vastly different separate works, continue
to blur the distinction by reference to "Sidney's *Arcadia,*" a title
appropriate only for the Countess of Pembroke's 1593 edition of
the *New Arcadia* supplemented by a slightly revised version of the
last three books of the *Old Arcadia*).

During 1580 and 1581, Philip and his father made their last
concerted assault on Elizabeth's conscience regarding the lot of
Sidneys, manqué in the royal service, but to no avail. Part of
Elizabeth's political strength lay in her ability to seem to grant
at the same time that she refused. There is no need to argue
whether or not after the events of 1579 Sidney was out of favor;
he was, right up to the moment of his death. This assertion is
hardly contradicted by the citation of exchanges of New Year's
gifts with the Queen and numbers of tournaments in which he

took part. These incidents merely indicate how Elizabeth could keep her courtiers busy without seriously employing them. In fact, when Sir Henry's final refusal of crown help came early in 1582, his son had just returned with the magnificent entourage that had escorted Anjou to his position in the Netherlands as the successor to Don John.

This progress is itself a larger example of Elizabeth's method of constantly counterbalancing each of her decisions. On the surface, the escort was provided for her future husband; in reality, it served to disguise the fact that for the third time Elizabeth was getting rid of "Monsieur," reversing her announced intention of marrying him. The disguise, furthermore, was not entirely a face-saving device; it led William of Orange to believe he was at last about to receive his long-sought aid from England. Although Elizabeth had refused to incorporate Holland and Zeeland in 1577, had not allowed Leicester to become governor-general of the federated Low Countries in 1578, nor allowed Sidney either to marry into Orange's family in 1577, to represent the crown in William's army in 1578, or to serve in Prince Casimir's armies in 1579, this apparent endorsement of Anjou served for a time at least as a delaying tactic. But Anjou proved a failure, was dismissed in 1583, and died in disgrace in 1584.

The death of Anjou, coupled with the shocking assassination of Orange and the discovery of the Throgmorton plot in the same year, finally forced Elizabeth to recognize that she must undertake direct steps to halt Spain, in the person of Parma, who was fast conquering the Low Countries. Short of English intervention, her resort was to encourage France to take over the leadership of the Dutch cause; she knew full well that the ill, childless Henry III was too busy trying to put down the Duke of Guise to be persuaded easily to open up a new front. For her ambassador to Paris, she turned to Sidney, a man whose temperament she now needed. Instructions were drawn and issued, and Sidney was at Gravesend awaiting favorable winds when word came canceling a mission which he could hardly have looked forward to, since he had no love for France and since he was a constant advocate of direct action. But, when Antwerp fell in 1585, England became so vulnerable that the Queen had to act; and Sidney's time at last came.

Sidney was fitted by prowess and by education to undertake the military governorship of Flushing, and not merely because of his activities on the Continent and in Ireland before 1580. In the years following these experiences, he had maintained his physical skills through tournaments and other equestrian exercise; and he also, more importantly, put his education to use by taking active roles in matters of defense, under his uncle Warwick, the Master of Ordinance, and in matters of foreign policy, under his father-in-law, Sir Francis Walsingham. As, so to speak, the assistant secretary of defense, Sidney's main duty was to oversee the arming of the Cinque Ports against probable Spanish invasion; as assistant secretary of state, his "desk" was Scotland; and as an extension of both jobs, he planned global strategy against Spain. In this last task, his never-realized idea was to escalate the naval piracy in the new world into actual amphibious raids against the diverse Spanish holdings.

The marriage negotiations between Sir Henry Sidney and Walsingham were begun probably some time in 1581 but were not concluded until March, 1583; and the marriage was then delayed because the Queen felt that her permission should have been sought earlier in the negotiations. The elder Sidney and Walsingham felt the matter was common knowledge. The Queen was still riding with tight rein on the Sidneys, although she was almost forced in 1582 to rely once more on Sir Henry to rule in Ireland and although she had knighted Philip in January. But the knighthood came not as a reward but only because Sidney's friend Prince Casimir had asked that Sidney stand proxy for him when he was installed at Windsor as a Knight of the Order of the Garter. The marriage stands out as strange by Elizabethan custom, for neither house gained materially from it. Sir Francis was proud of the fact that he valued Sidney as a person, and there is every indication that the relationship between Philip and his wife Frances was one based on love and trust. Walsingham, in fact, was ruined by the marriage; for, when Sidney died heavily in debt, he undertook to protect his son-in-law's name by satisfying all creditors. The Queen sat back and watched him lose his money and his health, then discharged him. Like his son-in-law, however, even in the face of death, Walsingham appeared with dignity and worth.

Sidney had in early letters from the Continent to Leicester, Burghley, Walsingham, and Languet showed great interest in foreign affairs or, more exactly, in international policy. Even after the death of Languet in 1581, as we know from Greville's *Life,* this interest was maintained and broadened to what we have seen was a global strategy. Sidney's letters of 1580 reflect the thrill which Englishmen felt when Sir Francis Drake returned from his circumnavigation—"about the world he hath bene, and rich he is returned." Sidney's name is found as subscriber to many expeditions, and in 1583 Hakluyt dedicated his first *Voyages* to Sidney. Sidney had encouraged the Queen to use the fleet not just to bring back booty and generally harass the Spanish; for, with Raleigh and others, he realized that England had a chance to strengthen her position in Europe through American colonization, a proposition which, to say the very least, struck most Elizabethans as nonsense. But Sidney had in mind a policy much more bold and far-reaching than the Queen's policy of balancing her enemies one against another—a policy that, as Mattingly has observed, she finally had to put aside in 1585 after the fall of Antwerp.[2]

Elizabeth wisely withheld her direct intervention in the Netherlands until the rebel states agreed to grant her the port cities of Flushing and Brill, which Warwick, as the Master of Ordinance, had warned would most logically be used by Parma as bases for his planned invasion of England. Furthermore, these cities were the main trade ports, ports of supply, for the provinces of Zeeland and Holland; and they controlled the main riverways into the Brabant and Flanders.

We can well imagine how pleased Sir Philip was when his name was mentioned in 1585 for the post of governor-general at Flushing even before arrangements were concluded. But the Queen played her usual game with Sidney; and, after Leicester was picked as military advisor to the provinces, she could not bring herself to decide between Burghley's son, Sir Thomas Cecil, or Sidney for Flushing. In the meantime, Sidney had been in conference with Drake, making plans for a fleet attack against Spanish shipping and holdings in the Indies. As the Dutch appointment seemed less and less likely, Sidney, either to force the Queen's hand or in a rash mood of indignation, decided to go along as commander of the landing forces in Drake's ships. When Sidney arrived secretly at Plymouth in September, Drake seems to have had second thoughts and to have informed the Queen of Sidney's intention. In short order, Drake was forbidden to allow Sidney to go aboard; and Sidney was notified that Cecil had been made governor of Brill and he, of Flushing.

V   *1585–1586: "We shall have a sore war uppon us this sommer"*

At long last Sidney was in the front lines, defending Queen and country in open warfare against Philip and Rome. His being in this important position fortunately brought a great deal of his correspondence into the official records, for these letters come as close as is historically possible to revealing the essential man: intelligent, good-hearted, principled, and, above all, energetic.

Because of the challenge implied in Sidney's giving the lie-direct to the gentle, loyal family servant Molyneux in 1578, the tennis-court argument with Oxford and the letter of marriage advice to the Queen in 1579, an allegedly self-consuming love affair in 1581, and the challenge to all comers offered in behalf of Leicester in 1584, we are apt to consider Sidney a Hotspur. As attractive as that Henry is, the other one, Prince and King Henry, is a more likely comparison. Like Hal, Sir Philip, underneath his *sprezzatura,* had a serious, meditative bent. Indeed, his friends from the beginning warned him of a tendency toward melancholy, and Wallace found his counterpart in the personality of Hamlet. But the same friends also testify that the presence of Sir Philip raised the spirits of any gathering and the sheer *energia* of his art is proof enough of his *joie de vivre.* This joy, like Hal's, is both intellectual and animal; for Sidney, too, seems to have taken as much delight in being the observer of, as in being the participant in, the comedy of life. Both men, finally, were daring in battle and trusted in God and country; but neither did so without prior metaphysical weighing and honest evaluation of the costs of war.

Sidney's deepest thoughts are not to be found, as Feuillerat suggested, in his art, but in his part of the translation of Du Plessis Mornay's treatise *The Truth of the Christian Religion,* published by Arthur Golding in 1587. Feuillerat first established at what point in the joint work Sidney turned the project over to Golding, but the difference is not just in style but in quality of mind. The tract is, in difficulty, halfway betwen Aquinas and Richard Hooker, and it is in the same tradition of argument from and to natural law. Sidney did not merely translate as did Golding; he grasped and recast each thought that made up one of the links in Mornay's chain of reasoning. Why Sidney left off the work is usually answered by citing Golding's dedication of the final work to Leicester in which he says that the call to the Netherlands forced Sidney to ask Golding to finish the work. But what is interesting is that Sidney's work stopped after a proof of God had been established, and his contribution can be seen again only in later chapters about the immortality of the soul—a subject of great concern to Sidney on his death bed. In other words, Sidney left to Golding the abstruse points of Protestant doctrine and was concerned with first principles, much as was Hooker in Book I of his *Laws of Ecclesiastical Polity,* before he settled down to specific discussion of Anglican Church polity. That Sidney turned the work over to Golding had nothing to do with the fact that he was going to war. Every soldier feels he will return home, and Sidney did not draw a will until after he was wounded.

Sidney's simple, but not fundamentalist or simplistic, faith, as well as his philosophical turn of mind, are seen repeatedly in his letters from Holland, especially so in a letter to Walsingham of March 24, 1586. The Queen has been reluctant to send her part of the soldiers' pay; Sidney knows that "I am called very ambitious and prowd at home," and he realizes from experience "how apt the Queen is to interpret every thing to my disadvantage." But Sidney does not whine:[3]

For me thinks I see the great work, indeed, in hand against the abusers of the world, wherein it is no greater fault to have confidence in man's power, than it is too hastily to despair of God's work. I think a wise and constant man ought never to grieve while he doth play, as a man may say, his own part truly, though others be out. But if himself leave his hold because other mariners will be idle, he will hardly forgive himself his own fault. For me, I cannot promise of my own course; no, . . . because I know there is a higher power that must uphold me, or else I shall fall. But certainly, I trust, I shall not by other men's wants be drawn from myself.

From his first arrival in Flushing, Sidney had been appalled by the condition of the English garrisons. Now that England was going to take direct charge of the "mercenaries," or "volunteers," that had been several years in the Netherlands, the Estates General refused to pay them; and Leicester had not yet arrived to take charge. Furthermore, in the vacuum that existed after the death of Orange, the abuses ever present in Medieval and Renaissance military pay systems (no worse than, or much different from, those still prevalent in twentieth-century Far Eastern armies) grew unchecked. The result was that nothing filtered down to the troops, who were forced to pillage and steal, which hardly endeared them to those whom they were there to defend. Sidney kept urging Leicester to hurry to his post so that reforms could be instituted. But Leicester was not the man Sidney had hoped he was: when he arrived, he squandered on himself and his immediate staff the money he received both from the Provinces and from England.

Leicester also made the situation worse by directly disobeying the Queen. He had been sent as a kind of senior military advisor, but he immediately agreed to become governor-general, replacing the eighteen-year-old son of William, Count Maurice, as governor, and the stormy Count Hohenlo as general. The Queen's anger was increased when she learned that he was being addressed as "Excellency" and had sent for his wife in order to set up a court. Sidney did not know that his uncle's new title was in contradiction to the Queen's written and oral instructions, but he had the good sense to write letters to England urging that Lady Leicester not be allowed in the Low Countries. Jealousy and needless expense were already sufficiently rampant to make Sidney despair of success in the coming campaigns: "We shall have a sore war uppon us this sommer, wherein if appointment had been kept and these disgraces forborn which have greatly weakened us we had been victorious" (III, 168).

Sidney was much in the field during the late spring and summer; for, in addition to the garrison of Flushing and a company of horse he had recruited in England, he had command of a regiment from Zeeland. The fact that he rallied the morale of his city and its garrison, had the loyal backing of all of his men, and was being considered as the governor of Zeeland is proof that he carried out all of his responsibilties with success. Indeed, before his death it was generally assumed that he would soon replace his aging and none-too-popular uncle. There is no direct evidence, however, that the Queen would have agreed, and her recollection that the honest government of Sir Henry Sidney in Ireland had been one of "great cost" to her could have brought about her veto. But two bits of evidence point the other way. Sidney's continued insistence that the English troops must get their pay finally seems to have reached her ears; for, after Leicester had established himself, her instructions to him begin to take up Sidney's refrain: attention must be paid to the poor soldier in garrison and camp. Perhaps Sidney's openness and honesty had finally registered with her. And certain it is from ample testimony that she was broken by the news of his death.

All of Europe, Catholic and Protestant alike, was stunned by the death of Sidney. Only thirty-two, he had by sixteenth-century experience reached middle life, but he still had a future ahead. The theme that reverberates through the countless messages of grief received by the Queen, Leicester, and Walsingham and the numerous epitaphs, elegies, and memorials in all languages is that of waste—of great expectations come to naught. The point was soberly captured by Fulke Greville: "What he was to God, his friends and country, fame hath told, though his expectation went beyond her good."[4] But he had lived long enough to establish his worth, to become the true representative of chivalry. Camden spoke what all instinctively felt: "Whatever we loved in you, whatever we admired in you still continues and will continue in the memories of men, the revolutions of ages, and the annals of time."[5] Perhaps the most moving tribute came from the humble professional soldier, George Whetstone. After enumerating Sidney's condition, education, lingual ability, foreign travel, martial achievement, and intimacy with "men of qualitie," he concluded with the simple assertion that "He alwaies was a speciall fauorer of Soldiers," a tribute moving because it comes from the ranks, and more so because Whetstone was himself in the lines at Zutphen on the September 22, 1586.[6]

VI   *"Ita venit in oculos hominum, ita excessit"*

How much Sidney did to plan the defense of England against the sure invasion by Spain is hidden behind the person of Warwick; what he did as Walsingham's agent to keep Scotland free is more easily ascertained; but how much he was able to help his father-in-law's protegé Drake is a matter of speculation. More clearly, his death reminded people that a man could live free under God if he had a sense of *virtue,* a sense of what it was to be a man, to be human—to think, to love, to do. He showed the world that a man need not cower, beg, lie, and obliterate his personality, his sense of self.

Still, the actual achievements of Sidney's life tend to be lost in the drama of his death. The famous stories told by Greville of the thigh-armor tossed aside before battle and of the canteen passed by the wounded captain to the dying soldier are fitting and probably true. But the acts suggest a man to whom life was a mere gesture and for whom each occasion should be a staged one, whereas the sense of *camaraderie* shown by the first act and the *noblesse* of the second reach deep into the man. In short, we lose Sidney when we romanticize him, just as the Renaissance tendency to moralize his life also obscured it.

Although each tendency is natural to each age, each isolates Sidney from his times and tends to make a statue of him. But surely he would not have enjoyed being Shaw's Commander, though possibly his Juan. Sidney, too, had a dream of the future, "the cause"—the forging of a Protestant League to destroy the vestiges of the Holy Roman Empire. England would lead, but not dominate; for Sidney did wish a Calvin-like substitution of a new tyranny for an old. Unlike Shaw's Juan, Sidney was content, however, with the institutions and potential of the present. His optimism was that of the Renaissance Humanist: God had ordered the world for man's benefit; and, even though man had lost his sense of that order through sin, God had allowed man to retain his right reason in order to work toward regaining a sense of that original order. Sidney's contribution toward achieving this future awareness lies somewhat in his life, more in his death, but mostly in his art, where we discover Sidney most fully. And through his art he made his most lasting contribution to the culture of the Renaissance—the most significant period in the civilization of the West.

CHAPTER 2

The Defence of Poesie

WHEN Greville said of Sidney that "his end was not writing, even while he wrote," he told enough of the truth to suit his purpose: to show that Sidney had totally dedicated his life to serving the crown in military and diplomatic affairs. The remark is just, for Sidney was not, any more than Greville, a "writer"; and Greville's *Life of Sidney* could be subtitled "Along with an Apology by the Author for His Having Written So Much." A "writer" was a professional, one who sold his work to printers. Sidney and Greville were amateurs who wrote to develop skills and pass the time. But the distinction is not so great as it might at first seem, (or as John Buxton would make it). The London literary circle contained professionals, semi-professionals, and amateurs; and it was sufficiently small to allow everyone in it to know what was "being done" and by whom. To be sure, the circle was class-structured; and, because it was part of society, all were not intimate: Shakespeare could dedicate a fashionable poem to the Earl of Southampton, but there is no indication before, and only a slight one after, that they more than merely knew of each other.

On the other hand, because all the members, regardless of "place," had in common a rhetorically based education, they shared the same assumptions concerning literary art, or "poesy," and were concerned alike with their medium, English. Sidney's major concern may not have been writing; but, when he wrote, his objective was to write well, both in form and content, or, to use his terms, in "manner" and "matter."

Although *The Defence of Poesie* may not have been completed until 1582, at least four years after Sidney had begun writing, it is the appropriate work with which to begin a consideration of Sidney's art; for its very form is a reminder that the *Defence* is a cumulative expression of theories and ideas to which Sidney had been exposed from grammar school on. Its particular inception may have been as early as his stay on the Continent, when he first read French and Italian critics; or it may have been in 1575, when he saw the lavish, but rather vapid "native" entertainment at Kenilworth; or in 1577, when Sidney began considering with Thomas Drant the possibilities and problems of imitating Latin quantity in English poetry, considerations which led to the experiments of Sidney, Greville, Dyer, Spenser, and Harvey in 1578 and 1579. Or the *Defence* may have been undertaken to tame the enthusiastic reaction to the appearance in December, 1578, of Lyly's *Euphues,* the style and patron of which, Ciceronianism and Oxford, respectively, were abhorrent to Sidney. For, whether or not his *Old Arcadia* was already in progress or was started in answer, it is consciously different from *Euphues.* The work on the *Old Arcadia,* both the books and eclogues, coupled with the conversations within the "Areopagus," are evidence enough that by 1580 Sidney was seriously concerned with the forms of literary art and with the enabling of English to express serious matter. Stephen Gosson's philistine *The School of Abuse* published in August, 1579, and surprisingly dedicated to Sidney, probably only served as a catalyst to bring Sidney to a formulation of his ideas because the *Defence* is not a point-for-point rebuttal of Gosson (Thomas Lodge did that in his *Reply* the same year). But even by the end of 1580 Sidney had not polished his ideas to the clarity which they have in the *Defence.*

A letter from Sidney to Robert Sidney in October states that the *Old Arcadia* was completed, and the same letter shows Sidney thrashing around for a philosophical justification for Robert's study of history (III, 130–33). Going to the root of the word "Historie", he says, "this I thinke in haste a story is either to be considered as a storie, or as a treatise which besides that addeth many thinges for profite and ornament." The story, then, is the formal narration of events along with their causes and results, all of which, by implication, teach, or instruct. But, when "the Historian makes himselfe a discourser [philosopher] for profite and an Orator, yea a Poet sometimes for ornament," he is able to accomplish more because as a philosopher he "speaks *non simpliciter de facto, sed de qualitatibus et circumstantis facti.*" This range beyond plain fact does more than merely teach; discussion of qualities and contexts can actually change or enrich the life of the reader. But a treatise can only be thus effectively meaningful either because, as an orator, the historian speaks through traditional forms, ones which the reader trained in rhetoric can easily follow, or because, as a poet, he paints forth "the effects, the motions, the whisperings of the people, which though in disputation one might say were true, yet who will marke them well shall finde them taste of a poeticall vaine, and in that kinde are gallantly to be marked, for though perchance they were not so, yet it is enough they might be so."

Sidney does not here pronounce the poet superior to the philosopher and historian, but he shows himself coming close to a conception of "poesy" as an imitation of nature—"it carrieth the life of a lively example"—which is able to teach, to move, and to delight. When he stated that the deeper, more rewarding historian adds profit and delight to his narration of fact, the way to the *Defence* was prepared; and the first step was taken when Sidney decided that writers such as Xenophon were not historians but poets. For the moment, however, he wrote "in greate haste, of method, without method, but with more leysure & studie (if I doe not finde some booke that satisfies) I will venter to write more largely of it unto yow."

In his leisure and study Sidney found many books which helped him clarify his ideas on learning, mainly those of Aristotle, Horace, Minturno, and Scaliger. But, after he had given the matter thought, he obviously concluded that none of these books would suffice; and he determined to write his own treatise.

I   *The* Defence *as Imitation*

After analyzing the "matter" of learning and studying how it most effectively could be attained, Sidney turned instinctively to the art of rhetoric for the proper manner for presenting his conclusions. George Puttenham defined art as "but a certaine order of rules prescribed by reason, and gathered by experience"; and Thomas Wilson defined rhetoric as "a learned, or rather an artificial, declaration of the minde in the handelyng of any cause, called in contention, that maie through reason largely be discussed."[1] The art of rhetoric, then, had its rules of procedure, its forms and traditions; but it also called for a play of intellect, for a display of individual talent. For this reason the study of rhetoric and the practice of disputation were at the heart of Tudor education, one which could be highly conservative, backward looking, and "Classical" in subject matter, yet liberal, forward looking, and "progressive" in manner. This education demanded that the student master a prescribed body of material which he in turn would exploit as he exercised his ingenuity in finding unique ways of displaying his learning. The point of juncture came within the principle of imitation, but the whole program of "Art, Imitation, and Exercise" (III, 37) could be literally self-defeating if exercise became subservient to art, a tendency seemingly encouraged by the nature of imitation.

Imitation was the manner in which a writer displayed learning, and it could be achieved by following one of two basic formulas. To use Ascham's rule of thumb, imitation was either similar treatment of dissimilar matter or dissimilar treatment of similar matter. An oration was an example of the first kind; and translation, because it was fresh handling of traditional matter, was imitation of the second kind but, as such, could reach the level of creative endeavor. Too often it did not, and Sidney could lament, "truly I could wish . . . the diligent Imitators of *Tully & Demosthenes,* most worthie to be imitated, did not so much keepe *Nizolian* paper bookes of their figures and phrases, as by attentive translation, as it were, devour them whole, and make them wholly theirs" (III, 42). These people displayed their art (they knew how to collect aphorisms and make comparisons, and had memorized the rules), but their exercise had been "fore-backwardly," which happens when, instead of exercising to know, "we exercise as having knowne: and so is our braine delivered of much matter, which never was begotten by knowledge" (III, 37). True learning demanded full understanding, and it needed, therefore, the exercise of the full man. Elizabethan students were not encouraged to be "original"—to be such was to be a fool—but to be genuine: to make what they learned "wholly theirs"; to digest it so totally that they could in turn act upon it.

This idea of integrity so lies behind and is so elaborated within the *Defence* that Sidney's treatise itself became an example of that which he was arguing in behalf of—"poesy." As an oration, the *Defence* is an imitation; and it could, as we might infer from Sidney's references to Cicero and Demosthenes, approach the level of poetry if the subject were well handled with regard both to art and exercise.

II   *The Art of the* Defence

Milton's *Areopagitica* is rightly great because the author had something to say which behooved mankind to remember—not because he displayed a mastery of a traditional form. So also with Sidney, but in both cases the art, or knowledge of the traditional rules, came first; and had these not been mastered in a way that kept the art hidden, the higher art would not have been apparent. Although Kenneth Myrick has demonstrated that the *Defence* follows the form of a Classical plea, or defense before the bar of justice, he tends to pass over what is ultimately more important: Sidney's contributions to esthetic theory and practical criticism.[2] Still, those contributions depend on the basic disposition of the material, and they must be approached through a full understanding of the disposition. Here, using Wilson's *Rhetorike* as a guide (and he may well have been Sidney's in writing the *Defence* just as he had been in person at Oxford in 1566), we can see how the seven parts of Sidney's oration follow one another and are related one to another.

First of all, Wilson reminds his reader what all speakers know by instinct: that the opening must be an attention getter, that by means of "the entraunce or beginning . . . the will of the standers-by, or of the Judge, is sought for, and required to heare the matter" (7). Sidney's *Exordium* (III, 3–4) is short and to the point at hand: "a pittiful defence of poore Poetrie." But in its tone is found, I think, the clearest evidence for Sidney's familiarity with Aristotle's *Rhetoric*.

Sidney had told Languet that he wanted to improve his Greek so that he could go directly to Aristotle instead of having to trust Latin translations; he recommended the *Ethics* and *Politics* to his brother Robert; and references to those works, as well as to the *Poetics,* appear in the *Defence*. But for evidence of Sidney's contact with the *Rhetoric,* there is only John Hoskyns's remark that Sidney had translated the first two books.[3] Aristotle in Books One and Three related the content of rhetoric to ethics and politics, and rhetorical style to poetry, referring his students to his other appropriate works. But in Book Two he emphasized that ultimate success in persuasion depends on the speaker, for it is he who must effectively blend content and style, being neither reporter nor pitch-man. To achieve the necessary balance, the speaker must know himself and his listeners; then he can establish an ethos ("voice" or "person") which will be convincing because it is drawn from within to meet the evaluated temper of the audience.

Sidney's concern with ethos is everywhere apparent in his art, so much so that Myrick has identified the concern as Castiglione's *sprezzatura,* or the studied casualness of the courtier. This attitude certainly is part of Sidney's literary art, that part which governs, appropriately, his view of the place in his life of his own writings —"his end was not writing"—and is present here: "[I,] who I know not by what mischance in these my not old yeares and idlest times, having slipt into the title of a Poet, am provoked to say something unto you in the defence of that my unelected vocation, which if I handle with more good will, then good reasons, beare with me." *Sprezzatura,* yes, but only as part of the ethos; for Sidney observed decorum, wearing the proper mask for each occasion. Although here the mask is almost no mask, the speaker being Sidney himself, the ethos is carefully established to serve the present need to disarm the reader.

Through the opening anecdote about the horseman Pugliano, amusing in itself, Sidney leads his audience to adopt toward him the same sense of amused but warm superiority which he held for the man who felt that horsemanship was the end of all life. Then he deftly creates an aura of sympathy for himself when, assuming that the reader will consider the exercise of poetry of more worth than horsemanship, he quickly closes the *Exordium* by lamenting that, while no one denies the "deserved credit" of horsemanship, even philosophers are defacing the name of poetry. This admission is no whimpering, for the resources and depth of the ethos are suggested even within this subtle use of pathos: the philosophers are, by implication, compared to children; and their art is put on a par with all other arts. Thus, if they keep up their bickering, there is "great daunger of civill warre among the Muses."

The smile slowly disappears as Sidney moves into his *Narratio,* "*And first truly . . .*" (III, 4–9). The way in which Wilson defined the narration as "a plain and manifest pointyng of the matter, and an evident settyng forthe of all thynges that belong unto the same, with a breef rehersal grounded upon some reason" (7) might have suggested to Sidney his exact outline for this section: first, there is a general description of the subject (III, 4–7); then, a specific statement of essential facts pertaining to the subject (III, 7–8); and, finally, an epitome of the argument (III, 8–9).

In his general description, Sidney plays the traditional orator; he gives the broad and respected history of his subject "which in the noblest nations and languages that are knowne, hath bene the first light giver to ignorance, and first nurse whose milke litle & litle enabled them to feed afterwards of tougher knowledges." But in his account he subtly begins his proof, for he asserts that the early poets were both historians and philosophers, able "to draw with their charming sweetnesse, the wild untamed wits to an admiration of knowledge." In short, poetry moves, delights, and instructs.

But Sidney moves slowly, continuing under the guise of historian, now as one of language: the Romans called the poet *Vates* or Prophet; the Greeks, based their noun on the verb *poiein,* from whence comes both the anglicized "poet" and directly translated "maker" of Middle English and Scots. By implication, the meeting point comes in Sidney's citation of the Psalms of David, a powerful proof in the Renaissance; for scholars of the new learning were trying to puzzle out the metrical rules by which they were made (Sidney's own translations should be kept in mind), yet one could hardly deny that the Psalms were prophetic, were divinely inspired. Like the pagan Oracles, they combined "that same exquisite observing of number and measure in the words, and that high flying libertie of conceit propper to the Poet." And again we have a statement sufficient for the present need, but one which prepares the way for Wilson's "evident settyng forthe" of essential aspects of the subject.

When Sidney makes the assertion that "there is no Art delivered unto mankind that hath not the workes of nature for his principall object, without which they could not consist, and on which they so depend, as they become Actors & Plaiers, as it were of what nature will have set forth," we might think he is bold because of our modern tendency to define art and nature psychologically. To Sidney, art was equivalent to "skill," a profession or craft to be learned and developed; and nature was the objective, empirical world. Therefore, his assertion merely implies that the techniques of ditch digging depend on the make-up of soils. But he does become bold as he continues: "onely the Poet disdeining to be tied to any such subjection, lifted up with the vigor of his own invention [subject or idea], doth grow in effect into an other nature." He does not depart from external nature, but goes "hand in hand with nature," for his works are "imitation" or "fiction." They are *made* from the materials of nature, but *shaped* by the artist's unique vision of something better than nature: "her world is brasen, the Poets only deliver a golden."

The vision is "imagined," but "is not wholly imaginative, as we are wont to say by them that build Castles in the aire"; the vision is grounded in nature, based upon reality. On the other hand, the poet's aim is not realism; he does not seek merely to reproduce exactly "a *Cyrus,* which had bene but a particular excellency as nature might have done, but to bestow a *Cyrus* upon the world to make many *Cyrusses,*"—a Cyrus real enough to have the stuff of life in him and ideal enough to inspire. But such art is not automatically efficacious; it demands the reader's awareness of the art of imitation through which "that maker made him."

Sidney uses the word "maker" in order to lead into his most daring statement in the whole *Defence,* one so central that it implies the whole argument:

Neither let it be deemed too sawcy a comparison, to ballance the highest point of mans wit, with the efficacie of nature: but rather give right honor to the heavenly maker of that maker, who having made man to his owne likenes, set him beyond and over all the workes of that second nature, which in nothing he sheweth so much as in Poetry; when with the force of a divine breath, he bringeth things foorth surpassing her doings: with no small arguments to the incredulous of that first accursed fall of *Adam,* since our erected wit maketh us know what perfection is, and yet our infected wil keepeth us from reaching unto it. (III, 8–9)

Sidney's definition of imagination lies behind Wordsworth's—"Reason in her most exalted mood"—and Keats's (with thanks to Milton), "We may liken the imagination to Adam's dream: he awoke and found it true." At the same time, the definition is logically based upon the sixteenth-century theological and physiological concept of "erected wit," or right reason—the divine attribute of man's rational soul and the source of poetic art.

Realizing that his narration had been elaborate (he used a high style) and assertive ("these arguments will by few be understood, and by fewer graunted"), Sidney slips back into his casual tone ("thus much I hope wil be given me, that the Greeks with some probability of reason, gave him the name above all names of learning") in order to make his transition to the presentation of proof ("now let us goe to a more ordinairie opening of him, that the truth may be the more palpable").

The giving of proof in a forensic oration falls into three parts: the *Propositio,* the *Divisio,* and the *Confirmatio.* In the *Defence,* the proposition is in perfect accord with Wilson's request for "a pithie sentence comprehended in a small roume the somme of the whole matter" (7): "*Poesie,* therefore, is an Art of *Imitation:* for so Aristotle termeth it in the word *Mimesis,* that is to say, a representing, counterfeiting, or figuring forth—to speake *Metaphorically,* a speaking *Picture*—with this end, to teach and delight" (III, 9).[4]

Once again, Wilson's definition, now of the division as "an openyng of thynges, wherein wee agree and reste upon, and wherein we sticke and stande in travers, shewyng what we have to saie in our owne behalfe" (7), could stand as the outline which Sidney used for his *Divisio* (III, 9–11). He immediately makes clear what is not under discussion, religious poetry, which, since inspired by the Holy Ghost, is too high, and descriptive poetry, which is too low since fidelity to the subject does not allow the poet "the free course of his own invention." The controversy centers, instead, on a third kind of poetry: that written by "right" poets, those who "most properly do imitate to teach & delight: and to imitate, borrow nothing of what is, hath bin, or shall be, but range onely reined with learned discretion, into the divine consideration of what may be and should be." These poets are both Makers and Seers. When the subject has been limited, Sidney then states his thesis: "these indeed do meerly make to imitate, and imitate both to delight & teach, and delight to move men to take that goodnesse in hand, which without delight they would flie as from a stranger; and teach to make them know that goodnesse wherunto they are moved."

Although Sidney then divides poetry into traditional types, he emphasizes that the ability to master a genre or to write in meter does not make a true poet; the noble end to which he writes does so. At the other extreme, however, Sidney, like Johnson later, painstakingly indicates that the end of poetry is not didactic, not mere teaching. Rather, true poetry possesses the mind and provides that deep delight which gives a full pleasure because its images of imitation answer the demands of both the spirit and the flesh. In Sidney's eyes, Xenophon's account of Cyrus is "an absolute heroicall Poeme"; Xenophon is a poet because "it is that faining notable images of vertues, vices, and what els, with that delightfull teaching, which must be the right describing note to know a Poet by." Still, Sidney is willing to narrow his defense to those who couch their matter "in that numbrous [numbered, proportioned] kind of writing which is called *vers*."

With this limitation established, Sidney is ready to begin the third part of the proof, the actual *Confirmatio* (III, 11–26), which itself falls into two parts: first, the weighing of poetry "by his workes [ends or accomplishments], and then by his parts [kinds]." These two paths had been indicated appropriately in the division, but the approach to the first had not been sufficiently cleared; for Sidney begins his confirmation with the statement of another assumption, all of which, by the book of rhetoric, should come in the narration or division. But the nature of this assumption has been repeatedly indicated before; and the clear annunciation of it here fits the immediate purpose of setting up the two "straw-men," the philosopher and the historian.

Sidney assumes—and it would be hard to fault him on philosophical, theological, or psychological grounds, in his age or ours —that the end of life is the fullest, richest development of the human being. In his terms "the finall end is, to lead and draw us to as high a perfection, as our degenerate soules made worse by their clay-lodgings, can be capable of." The means of fulfillment is through "purifying of wit, . . . enriching of memorie, enabling of judgement, and enlarging of conceit," all of which he simply calls learning. Regardless of the number of disciplines dedicated to learning, all have the same end: "to know, & by knowledge to lift up the minde from the dungeon of the bodie, to the enjoying his owne divine essence." Although most branches of learning end only in specialized knowledge, they still subserve "the highest end of the mistresse knowledge[,] by the Greeks [called] *Arkitecktonic,* which stands as I thinke, in the knowledge of a mans selfe, in the Ethike and Politique consideration, with the end of well doing, and not of well knowing onely."[5] In sum, "the ending end of all earthly learning being verteous action, those skils that most serve to bring forth that, have a most just title to be Princes over al the rest." With this statement, the stage is set for the re-enactment of the ancient debate among the philosopher, the historian, and the poet.

Sidney concedes that the lore of the philosopher has the potential to move man because it is full of undoubted good, but "his knowledge standeth so upon the abstract and generall, that happie is that man who may understand him, and more happie, that can apply what he doth understand." The philosopher's art, therefore, can "neither strike, pearce, nor possesse the sight of the soul"; it cannot satisfy "inward conceit, with . . . a true lively knowledge"; his precepts lie "darke before the imaginative and judging power"; they cannot "inhabit both the memory and judgement." In short, philosophy is not vivid enough to engage and hold attention.

History is, of course, vivid, as Sidney grants; but the historian "is so tied, not to what should be, but to what is, to the particular truth of things, and not to the general reason of things, that his example draweth no necessary consequence, and therefore a lesse fruitful doctrine." Naturally, the poet has the best of both worlds: "whatsoever the *Philosopher* saith should be done, he [the poet] gives a perfect picture of it by some one, by whom he presupposeth it was done, so as he coupleth the generall notion with the particular example."

Repeating his assumption that "vertue is the most excellent resting place for al worldly learning," Sidney crowns poetry as the winner for "being the most familiar to teach it, and most Princely to move towards it." He then turns to the second part of the confirmation, the neo-Classical defense by kinds (III, 22–25), throughout which he weaves the theme of poetry's ability to teach and to move, along with the suggestion of a theme which becomes the burden of the *Confutatio:* any weakness to be found is not in the art of poetry but in the practitioners.

After a full summary of the arguments presented so far, both in the narration and in the confirmation (III, 25–26), Sidney turns to the *Confutatio* (III, 26–35). Because the confutation is a kind of rebuttal of the charges made by the prosecution, the speaker must exercise at this point all of his oratorical skill. He should be confident, witty, and mildly contemptuous of the opposition, all of which Sidney delightfully is. Because Sidney had undertaken to defend poetry in its traditional forms, his first specific defense is of "ryming and versing," even though he reminds us that "it is not ryming and versing that maketh *Poesie:* One may be a *Poet* without versing, and a versefier without *Poetrie.*" Nevertheless, Sidney here defines more fully an attribute of poetry that has been touched upon previously: its ability to give delight. So far, most emphasis has been on teaching and moving—on the "matter"—but subtending and framing the matter is the "manner," or the specific art of poetry which gives words their "number, measure, order, [and] proportion," thus, in short, affording "their delight." Sidney's emphasis on "Harmonie," that innate desire to have things "sweet and orderly," to have everything in place and pleasing to the senses, may have been encouraged by Aristotle's discussion of *harmonia* in the *Poetics.* Indeed, Sidney may also have drawn upon Aristotle's concept of the instinct for imitation (not to be confused with the Renaissance definition) for his additional observation that rhyme and measure are the best aids for memory, "the onely handle of knowledge."

After this defense of the manner of poetry, Sidney turns to the four "most important imputations laid to the poore *Poets*": that reading poetry is a waste of time, that poetry "is the mother of lyes," that it is a decadent in itself, and that Plato banished the poets from his Commonwealth, which last "they cry out with open mouth as if they had overshot *Robinhood.*" The first charge depends on the question at hand: if poetry effectively moves, teaches, and delights (all together), then the study and practice of it is most worthwhile. The second charge depends on semantics: the dual definition of fiction. If to lie is to try to pass off as literally true that which is actually not true, then poetry is innocent; for its fabrication simply is. Lines on a page and movements on a stage may be accepted or rejected, but their existence has nothing to do with truth or falsehood; they simply *are.* Poetry is made; it is a fiction. Because fiction is projected from the mind of the poet, because it is imaginative, the word has the connotation of "not true." But fiction only stands for life, is a reading of life, and can be lifelike; it does not pretend to *be* life: "What childe is there, that coming to a play, and seeing *Thebes* written in great letters upon an old doore, doth beleeve that it is Thebes?" Poetry is imaginative, in its source and in its appeal.

Sidney's answer to the third charge is related to his answer to the second, although he does not overtly make the connection. Throughout the *Defence,* and just now, he has defined poetry as an art of imitation, as a man-made projection, as "*eikastic*"; therefore, it follows that poetry cannot abuse "mans wit, but that mans wit abuseth *Poetrie* . . . . Nay truly, though I yield, that *Poesie* may not onely be abused, but that being abused by the reason of his sweete charming force, it can do more hurt than anie other armie of words." Once the force of poetry is granted, however, it must further follow that "being rightly used" poetry does "most good." As a result, "in this their argument of abuse, they proove the commendation."

In answering the fourth charge Sidney takes great pleasure in pointing out, in general, that all the great philosophers had a touch of the poet and specifically that Plato banished the poets because he recognized the powerful appeal of poetry to the mind of man. In fact, Plato "attributeth unto *Poesie,* more then my selfe do; namely, to be a verie inspiring of a divine force, farre above mans wit." Thus, by means of a clever reminder of Sidney's own special definition of inspiration in the *Narratio,* Plato is enlisted among the defenders; and Sidney concludes the confutation with a summary of his answers to the four objections.

Before entering into the seventh phase of his oration, the *Peroratio,* Sidney launches into a long *digression* (III, 35–45), a move justified and recommended by Aristotle and others, but not numbered among the parts of an oration for the plain reason that it is what it is: a digression. Nevertheless, the effective orator used his digression as a means of summarizing his case indirectly and of reaffirming his ethos before resting his case. Sidney's practical criticism of the state of poetry in England deserves separate consideration elsewhere in this study, but it should be noted that this criticism is connected with the esthetic theory being developed: "England the Mother of execellent mindes" should bring forth excellent poets, "who certainly in wit ought to passe all others, since all onely proceedes from their wit, beeing indeed makers of themselves, not takers of others." Then the seventh part, the actual conclusion, links English poetry with poetry in general.

The *Peroratio* (III, 45–46) is a single, summary charge to "all that have had the evill luck to read this inck-wasting toy of mine, even in the name of the nine *Muses,* no more to scorne the sacred misteries of *Poesie.*" The whole range of Sidney's literary ethos is present—*sprezzatura* on the surface; serious commitment beneath: "but if (fie of such a but) you bee borne so neare the dull-making *Cataract* of *Nilus,* that you cannot heare the Planet-like Musicke of *Poetrie*; if you have so earth-creeping a mind that it cannot lift it selfe up to looke to the skie of *Poetrie,* . . . thus much Curse I must send you in the behalfe of all *Poets,* that while you live, you live in love, and never get favour, for lacking skill of a Sonet, and when you die, your memory die from the earth for want of an Epitaphe."

III   *The* Defence *as Esthetic Theory*

The very fact that Sidney would undertake a formal defense shows his serious commitment to art, but the fact that it is a formal defense tends to obscure the esthetic theory which is woven throughout. By focusing on the parts of the defense, we tend to miss the very simple but profound conceptions of art and of the artist which inform Sidney's poetic.

The prime attribute of poetry is that it affords delight. Its formal characteristics such as number, duration, balance, and order appeal to our instinctive search for *harmonia;* and its relation to the facts of life satisfies our innate desire to know, or "to adjust to our environment." Thus, the manner of poetry is directed toward our physical side, but it depends for its relative effectiveness on the poet's ability to exercise within the rules of his craft; and the matter is directed to the mind, but depends for its effectiveness not just on the magnitude or seriousness of the subject at hand but also on the poet's ability to grasp and handle the subject. The delight of manner stimulates; the delight of matter instructs. To Sidney it is "manifest, that the *Poet* with that same hand of delight, doth draw the mind more effectually then any other Art" (III, 21).

This power of the poet to move men is reiterated throughout. From the casual, "Certainly I must confesse mine owne bar-barousnesse, I never heard the old Song of *Percy* and *Duglas,* that I founde not my heart mooved more then with a Trumpet; and yet is it sung but by some blinde Crowder, with no rougher voyce, then rude stile" (III, 24). To the more studied, the poet "begin-neth not with obscure definitions, which must blurre the margent with interpretations, and loade the memorie with doubtfulnesse: but hee commeth to you with words set in delightfull propor-tion, either accompanied with, or prepared for the well enchanting skill of *Musicke,* and with a tale forsooth he commeth unto you, with a tale, which holdeth children from play, and olde men from the Chimney corner" (III, 19-20). And, to the openly philosophical, true poets "make to imitate, and imitate both to delight & teach, and delight to move men to take that goodnesse in hand, which without delight they would flie as from a stranger; and teach to make them know that goodnesse wherunto they are moved; which being the noblest scope to which ever any learning was directed, yet want there not idle tongues to barke at them" (III, 10).

This last passage has more to do with the poet than with poetry, but art and artist are connected through Sidney's insistence that poetry is *eikastic*—is man made. The poet is a maker; he imitates. He takes the stuff of life, molds it, and projects it as art, as artifact. Unlike Plato, Sidney denies the concept of the poet in a fine frenzy; but he is more "Platonic" than Aristotle since Sidney shows less dependency on external nature. The reason is simple to find: Sidney was a Christian, a term which raises fear, confusion, anger, and even embarrassment in our Western world which is, nevertheless, as Harry Golden likes to remind us, historically and presently "Christian." Regardless of personal orientation, we should be able to understand that for Sidney, as for Milton, the Bible contained literal truth. To them it was an established fact that man experienced a fall from grace, a separation from good, a loss of contact with perfection—and that his whole history has been a struggle to regain his former vision of wholeness. Because man's speculation remained inexact and fanciful until the Word was revealed, while his essential nature remained constant since Adam, all myths found their true analogues in Scripture. To say that these myths were "replaced" by Scripture would imply a historic sense that the sixteenth century had not developed.

Man simply had lived in two periods—prelapsarian and postlapsarian; and the second was divided between pre-Christian and Christian. Although the spiritually deprived pagans sometimes had lived better lives under their myths (witness Aeneas), still the sixteenth century did not divide to argue the ancients versus the moderns. Christianity did not change man's nature; it only offered him the means of improving that nature. Thus, life itself was neither better nor worse than before, but it was immensely more challenging. Man was no longer hopelessly doomed, but could work to remove the burden of the curse and hope to achieve the sweet fruition of a heavenly crown; for, to repeat, "the finall end is, to lead and draw us to as high a perfection, as our degenerate soules made worse by their clay-lodgings, can be capable of" (III, 11). Man *is* capable, but the way is not easy, "since our erected wit maketh us know what perfection is, and yet our infected will keepeth us from reaching unto it" (III, 9). Man must be enticed, must be moved to know and to do what he is capable of. For the poet, *"hoc opus, hic labor est"* (III, 19).

The poet moves not because he is a prophet blessed, but because he is a man speaking to other men through an appeal to their common nature and their common experience. Relying on his God-given reason, the poet can discover (fr. *inventio*) meaningful relationships among the data of that experience, connections which he then reveals to other men. By trusting his imagination the poet achieves insight; the poet, "disdeining to be tied to any . . . subjection [to nature], lifted up with the vigor of his own invention, doth grow in effect into an other nature: . . . freely raunging within the Zodiack of his owne wit" (III, 8). Nature is fallen and cursed, but man is only partially her creature, for he is created in the divine image, which sets "him beyond and over all the workes of that second nature" (III, 8). He carries "the force of a divine breath" within him, which lifts him from nature. The poet exercises this ordering, creative power within him when he fashions his imitations of nature. From Sidney, the step to Coleridge's "repetition in the finite mind of the eternal act of creation in the infinite I AM" seems short; but to Sidney the poet stands between God and second nature, whereas Coleridge gives nature the intermediary position. But the terminology is justly shared, as is both critics' return to the principle of *architectonic*.

Sidney would be quick to agree with Johnson and Coleridge that the purpose of poetry is not to teach, but to give pleasure— not merely the titillating pleasure of the rare device, a pleasuredome with caves of ice, but the deep delight of the song which can imply the limited, deliberately inhuman vision of a Kubla Khan at the same time that it describes his achievements. Because poetry is the art of uniting pleasure with truth, it can possess the reader; and most laymen, in defense, will always want to weave protective circles thrice around the poet.

This kind of ultimately serious realization on Sidney's part of the power of poetry makes the *Defence* such a remarkable document. Sidney fully realized that his theories would "by few be understood, and by fewer graunted." He realized that Gosson's cry was not really so much directed against plays or poetry, but was part of "a chain-shot against all learning or bookishnes, as they commonly terme it" (III, 31). To Sidney, the life of the mind was essential to truly living; "it is manifest that all government of action is to be gotten by knowledge, and knowledge best, by getting manie knowledges, which is reading" (III, 31). But Sidney's is no academic discourse: *architectonic* stands "in the knowledge of a mans selfe, in the Ethike and Politique consideration, with the end of well doing, and not of well knowing onely" (III, 11).

Today the idea of well doing tends to imply our doing good for the sake of goodness. To Sidney, goodness simply meant being true to our human potential. Indeed, the Renaissance gloried in the false etymology of virtue, finding its stem in *vir:* to become virtuous was to effectively develop one's positive human qualities through exercise of one's uniquely human characteristic—reason. Machiavelli and Montaigne each in his own way laughed at such a philosophy; but being true to self could be an ideal, not a pragmatic, and a theocentric, not a homocentric, philosophy so long as goodness meant naturalness in the Aristotelian, Aquinian tradition. The personal and social efficacy of such a tradition was so obvious to Sidney (the ideals of his art are proof of it) that we find it nowhere referred to in the *Defence,* although it is assumed throughout.[6] Thus it is further assumed, to use Milton's phrasing and Sidney's term, that he who would be a "right poet" must himself be a right poem. The poet must fully know himself and his art in order to be true to both.

Initially, those tempted to write poetry should "looke themselves in an unflattering glasse of reason" to honestly determine if they have the special gift; even though "all other knowledges lie readie for anie that have strength of wit: A *Poet* no industrie can make, if his owne *Genius* be not carried into it." But Sidney is quick to add "that as the fertilest ground must be manured, so must the highest flying wit have a *Dedalus* to guide him" (III, 37). All learning demands a play of intellect but poetry demands the fullest —demands the exercise of reason in her most exalted mood.

Poetry is a valid branch of learning, for it is a mode of growth. Through the practice of Art, Imitation, and Exercise, the poet's wit is sharpened; and, as it is sharpened, it becomes a more effective tool for the discovery of the essential relationships and qualities of nature which are hidden beneath the "second nature" of everyday reality. Through this ever-building process, each succeeding imitation becomes "better"—more engaging and revealing, not of the poet, but of life through the poet. As Henry James observed, all great art bears the impress of the mind of the artist, and his own is not only a case in point, but a healthy reminder that the mind of the author can be everywhere apparent and the man remain perfectly hidden. To clench the point, we need only mention Shakespeare.

Thus, to Sidney, the most effective poem has an engaging "forciblenesse or *Energia,* (as the Greeks call it of the writer)" (III, 41), which we call artistic integrity. The literary ethos of the writer becomes the ethos of the work, the basis of its delight, the force of its persuasion, and the means of its instruction. Because of the doctrine of imitation, the work is not the writer; the work belongs equally to the writer and the reader since it is the marriage of art and nature. The writer's handling of imitation gives the work of art both its objective existence and its lifelike appearance: it demands "the right use both of matter and manner" (III, 43). Judging by this esthetic, Sidney "found in divers smal learned Courtiers, a more sound stile, then in some professors of learning, of which I can gesse no other cause, but that the Courtier following that which by practise he findeth fittest to nature, therein (though he know it not) doth according to art, thogh not by art: where the other using art to shew art and not hide art (as in these cases he shuld do) flieth from nature, & indeed abuseth art" (III, 43). These courtly writers balanced Art, Imitation, and Exercise.

Because of such a doctrine, or program, Renaissance art is highly conventional; for the artist was fully aware of what had been done before. Furthermore, there are emergent in the sixteenth century signs of a neo-Classicism as the natural outgrowth of the Medieval love of categories applied to the renaissant interest in ancient letters. And because of Sidney's well-known strictures on native drama and Joel Spingarn's dismissal of the *Defence* as a mere restatement of Italian criticism, we tend to assume that Sidney was the first English neo-Classical critic. But Sidney, even in his criticism and surely in his art, mostly paid lip service to the doctrine of pure genre. Generic terms in the sixteenth century

marked pedagogical, not artistic, categories. They were useful
critical pointers, not artistic absolutes.

To be sure, Sidney lists in his *Divisio* the "most notable" sub-
divisions of "right" poetry as "the *Heroick, Lyrick* [Great Ode],
Tragick, Comick, Satyrick, Iambick, Elegiack, Pastorall" (and
those are indeed the categories, in reverse order, which he dis-
cusses in the second half of his *Confirmatio*). But he continues in
the *Divisio*—"and certaine others: some of these being tearmed
according to the matter they deale with, some by the sort of verse
they liked best to write in"; and he adds that not all poetry is even
in verse. Then he prefaces his discussion by types in the *Confirmatio* with: "Now in his parts, kindes, or *species,* as you list to
tearme them, it is to be noted, that some *Poesies* have coupled
togither two or three kindes, as the *Tragicall* and *Comicall,* where-
upon is risen the *Tragicomicall,* some in the maner have mingled
prose and verse, as *Sanazara* and *Boetius*; some have mingled
matters *Heroicall* and *Pastorall,* but that commeth all to one in
this question, for if severed they be good, the conjunction cannot
be hurtfull" (III, 22).

The point should be clear that Sidney was interested in a variety
of qualities and not rigorously defined categories, as were the
Italian critics. The "right use of matter and manner" is centered
in the artist, not in the rules of his art. Sidney was as insistent as
T. S. Eliot that the artist must fully "devoure" tradition and make
it wholly his.

IV   *The* Defence *as Practical Criticism*

This obligation of serious dedication is clearly the theme which
dominates in the digression on the current state of poetry in England (III, 35–45). At the very outset, Sidney emphasized that the
traditional independence and self-reliance of the English—"makers
of themselves, not takers of others"—establish them as qualified
to be poets. But he soon laments that the English do not rely upon
and develop their "excellent mindes": "Exercise indeed we do,
but that verie fore-backwardly; for where we should exercise to
know, we exercise as having knowne: and so is our braine delivered of much matter, which never was begotten by knowledge.
For there being two principall parts, Matter to be expressed by
words, and words to expresse the matter: In neither, wee use Art
or imitation rightly. Our matter is, *Quodlibet,* indeed though

wrongly performing, *Ovids* Verse. *Quicquid conabor dicere, Versus erit:* never marshalling it into anie assured ranck, that almost the Readers cannot tell where to finde themselves" (III, 37).

To Sidney, the experience of the poet is all important; it leads to his grasp of matter, giving him something worthwhile to say. With but the few exceptions of Chaucer's *Troilus and Creseyde,* Surrey's poems, *A Mirror for Magistrates,* and Spenser's *Shepheardes Calender,* Sidney suggests that prose paraphrases of all published English poetry would uncover "a confused masse of words . . . barely accompanied with reasons" (III, 38). Poetry is on the wane in England because "base men with servill wits undertake it, who thinke it inough if they can be rewarded of the Printer" (III, 36).

When Sidney reviewed the published output of poetry in the early 1580s, he did not have much in quantity to deal with, though we might feel there was more quality poetry than he mentioned. Of those writers he cites all were available: the Chaucer edition of 1532 had been reissued in 1561, *A Mirror for Magistrates* (1559) had appeared in its latest form in 1578, the *Songes and Sonettes, written by Henry Howard, late Earle of Surrey and others* (1557) had reappeared for the fifth time in 1574 (and would again in 1585), and the *Shepheardes Calender* had been the publishing sensation of late 1579. The most significant poet of the 1570s, George Gascoigne, Sidney does not mention—nor Barnaby Googe, George Turburvile, Nicholas Breton, or Thomas Howell (who was employed by his sister), but each of these had written respectable poems. Thomas Churchyard and George Whetstone (ironically) Sidney probably felt to be beneath his regard. On the other hand, some poems by Edward de Vere, the Earl of Oxford, had appeared in Richard Edwards' *Paradise of Dainty Devises* (1576) and in Thomas Proctor's *Gorgeous Gallery of Gallant Inventions* (1578), collections worthily modeled on the successful Tottel's "Miscellany" (1557); but Sidney seems to have been amused by the fact that a nobleman had stooped to the folly of print:

while in the meane time, they *Queis meliore luto finxit præcordia Titan,* are better content to suppresse the out-flowings of their wit, then by publishing them, to be accounted Knights of the same order. But I that before ever I durst aspire unto the dignitie, am admitted into the companie of the *Paper-blurrers,* do finde the verie true cause of our wanting estimation, is want of desert, taking uppon us to be *Poets,* in despite of *Pallas.* Now wherein we want desert, were a thank woorthie labour to expresse. But if I knew I should have mended my selfe, but as I never desired the title, so have I neglected the meanes to come by it, onely over-mastered by some thoughts, I yeelded an inckie tribute unto them. (III, 36)

Myrick's interpreting this last sentence as *sprezzatura* misses the joke: Sidney is laughing at a nobleman who sought the title of poet by joining the "company" of poets ("aspire into the dignity" being good craft terminology). Once again Sidney objects to a writer's going through the motions of poetry without presenting the substance. Even the praise of the self-consciously presented work of Sidney's literary protegé Edmund Spenser is hedged about: "The Sheepheards Kalender, hath much *Poetrie* in his Egloges, indeed woorthie the reading, if I be not deceived. That same framing of his style to an olde rusticke language, I dare not allow: since neither *Theocritus* in Greeke, *Virgill* in Latine, nor *Sanazara* in Italian, did affect it" (III, 37).

Sidney's view of the English scene can easily be misunderstood as a kind of courtly aloofness. Certainly his treatment of native drama has all the perversity of the worst sort of academic criticism. But to dismiss his observations of the drama as merely nascent neo-Classicism is to miss his utter seriousness regarding the essential nature of poetry: "But I have lavished out too many words of this Play-matter; I do it, because as they are excelling parts of *Poesie,* so is there none so much used in England, and none can be more pittifully abused: which like an unmannerly daughter, shewing a bad education, causeth her mother *Poesies* honestie to be called in question" (III, 41). After this eloquent plea for integrity regarding "matter"—poetic drama and the writing of lyrics—Sidney turns to "manner," but the burden remains the same: the need to develop and maintain integrity.

When Sidney defined the outside of poetry as "words, or (as I may tearme it) *Diction,*" he moved beyond "Versifiers" to castigate as well "Prose-Printers" such as Lyly, the grammarians of both Oxford and Cambridge, and the Cambridge-trained ministers whose extreme Ciceronianism struck Sidney as running counter to the natural development of the vernacular, and hence the purpose of art: the imitation of nature. Writers such as Lyly were so consciously artificial that they could not move: "they obtaine an opinion of a seeming finenesse, but perswade few, which should be the ende of their finenesse" (III, 42). And Sidney's analysis of Lyly's style is masterful: "Now for similitudes in certain Printed discourses, I thinke all Herberists, all stories of beasts, foules, and fishes, are rifled up, that they may come in multitudes to waite upon any of our conceits, which certainly is as absurd a surfet to the eares as is possible. For the force of a similitude not being to prove any thing to a contrary disputer, but onely to explaine to a willing hearer, when that is done, the rest is a moste tedious pratling, rather overswaying the memorie from the purpose whereto they were applied, then anie whit enforming the judgement alreadie either satisfied, or by similitudes not to be satisfied" (III, 42–43).

True persuasion can come in oratory only when the ethos of the speaker wins the hearer; in poetry, when the ethos of the poem possesses the reader. And such persuasion is possible in either case only when the author honestly follows the natural principles of language: "doth according to art, thogh not by art." To Sidney, English was perfectly suited "for the uttering sweetly and properly the conceit of the minde, which is the end of speech" (III, 44).

Sidney did not have to engage in the problem of vernacular over Latin art. That battle, or skirmish, was easily won by Elyot, Cheke, Ascham, Wilson, and the rest; and theirs was an especially easy victory because, in this the pedagogic issue, the side of the vernacular was supported by the concern of the Reformation to make the word of God directly available to the people. But the narrower problem of vernacular poetry was not so settled, and the specter of Latin was not so easily exorcised.

Poetry by Sidney's own definition was "that numbrous kind of writing which is called *vers*"; and, Sidney jumped into the middle of a critical battle when he began the last section of his digression with the casual assertion: "Now of versefying, there are two sorts, the one, auncient, the other moderne. The auncient marked the quantitie of each sillable, and according to that, framed his verse: The moderne, observing onely number, with some regard of the accent; the chiefe life of it, standeth in that like sounding of the words, which we call Rime." To the sixteenth century there were two kinds of poetry: verse and rime. Verse was Latin, cultured and exact, its "art" having been long established and consciously followed, by Virgil as well as by the youngest sixteenth-century schoolboy; rime was vernacular, native and varied, its "art" differing in each county and followed with relative degrees of awareness of structural principles.

Here, in the early 1580s, Sidney straddled the fence in this debate of ancient versus modern: "truly the English, before any Vulgare language, I know is fit for both sorts" (III, 44). As early as 1576, he was sought out by Drant, the great champion of quantitative measure in English; and his own earliest poetry contains a variety of quantitative experiments. But later he seems to have learned, as I hope to show, that following number and duration would not allow English to sing, whereas following number and accent would: in *Astrophel and Stella,* as John Thompson observes, "the metrical system of modern English reaches perfection for the first time" (139).

V   *The Achievement of the* Defence

Sidney's *Defence of Poesie* is the perfect fruition of his education, at the center of which was the study of rhetoric, framed by grammar and logic. In assessing his achievement, I shall turn again to Wilson, who said that there are five things to be considered in evaluating an orator: his invention of matter, disposition of the matter, elocution, memory, and utterance. Utterance has to do with ethos, the "framyng of the voyce, countenaunce, and gesture after a comely maner" (6), whether in speaking or writing. Ethos, of course, goes much deeper, depending indeed on all five things equally; but, unless attention is paid to utterance, the other matters are apt to fall flat, the speaker becoming merely a neutral medium. But Sidney's balance of genial wit and high seriousness engage the attention throughout his presentation of the *Defence.*

In many ways his display of "memory" is the most impressive part, but this aspect I have not emphasized because it has been so thoroughly established by scholars. Memory was the use of learning, the having of names, facts, precedents, as well as of words, schemes, and figures of speech readily at hand. Sidney's education called for thorough if not wide reading in the Classics and commentators on them, which he supplemented by delving into "modern" literature, creative as well as critical, Ariosto as well as Castelvetro, all of which knowledge is fully but casually used throughout the *Defence.*

Turning to invention, disposition, and elocution is turning to the *trivium*; for elocution stems from accomplishment in grammar (composition or exposition, as we would call it), disposition (essential to an imitation) is the backbone of rhetoric, and invention (finding and analyzing a topic) depends on logic. Wilson's phrase "invention of matter" can suggest "making something up"—if we forget that invention to Sidney meant the discovery or uncovering of a truth that exists in nature or beyond nature. The "matter" to be analyzed here was poetry, and he discovered that its essential nature was *eikastic* and its essential characteristic was that it could reach out and possess; poetry proceeded from the nature of man as a rational animal and, in turn, appealed to that complex nature.

Sidney's invention is, then, the heart of the *Defence,* that from which the *Defence* proceeds and that which raises it close to the level of "poesy." For the "manner" of his imitation, Sidney took the deliberative oration; for the "matter," his own conception of poetry. That the conception is not self-contained or unique is to be expected, for Sidney would have believed it foolish not to base his work on the wisdom and insights of others. But the conception is in its final form genuine, wholly his. It is in the end the kind of thing he feels a great poem should be: alive, possessing, and persuasive. The art by which it is arranged is hidden behind the artless pose of the speaker, yet the speaker does not call such attention to himself that his subject is obscured. His *energia* informs the subject; and we come away fully convinced that, even if we cannot all be poets, at least we know what a poem is: a unique apprehension of experience made engagingly comprehensible.

Since the bond between poet and reader is their common God-given nature, it follows that poetry should be a power for good, but it also follows that it can be a diabolical power, for man's nature can best be understood as having suffered the nature of an insurrection. The right use of "matter" and "manner" ultimately depends on invention. Gascoigne felt that "the first and most necessarie poynt that ever I founde meete to be considered in making a delectable poeme is this, to grounde it upon some fine invention . . . some good and fine devise, shewing the quicke capacitie of a writer; and where I say some good and fine invention, I mean that I would have it both fine and good."[7]

Sidney surely knew Gascoigne; but, since he was a leading member of the "companie of *Paper-blurrers*," Sidney took little notice of him. But he surely would have agreed with Gascoigne's assertion; for it is that of the *Defence*. And we can say as well that it aptly describes the *Defence*.

CHAPTER 3

The Lady of May *and*
Old Arcadia

I   The Lady of May

GEORGE GASCOIGNE "devised and penned" much of the pseudo-dramatic pageantry through which Leicester entertained and flattered the Queen in July, 1575; and he was in residence at Kenilworth at the end of her long stay, for he was called upon at the last minute to provide a "farewell." Sidney may have met him then, but he surely knew of him. Of good family and trained as a lawyer, Gascoigne was one of England's first "professional" writers, a man who wrote for hire and who sought to have his work published—facts which placed him outside the pale of Sidney's circle. Although Sidney nowhere mentions his name, Gascoigne's literary efforts and achievements could well have stimulated Sidney's own: Gascoigne's highly explorative and experimental poetry provides a link between Wyatt's and Sidney's, his "Master F.J." is a pioneering step toward the novel, his "Certayne notes" are a remarkably acute and stimulating series of critical remarks on native poetics, and his *Supposes* and *Jocasta* are the first English adaptations of Italian plays. Especially in the "farewell" to the Queen which he provided Leicester, Gascoigne reminded Sidney what was expected in royal entertainment; and he may even have provided him with a suggestion of theme and characterization for *The Lady of May*, Sidney's first public, non-academic literary gesture.

Written probably for the visit of Elizabeth in May, 1578, to Wanstead, the manor house near Greenwich, which, like Kenilworth was a gift of hers to Leicester, *The Lady of May* has the same kind of "spontaneous" quality and ultimate purpose as had Gascoigne's entertainment. But Sidney's shows as well his reliance on his academic background in general, and specifically so in his imitation of an Italian form of drama: the *commedia rusticale*.

Sidney while on his grand tour may well have watched performances of this popular kind of farce, which is derived from the *contrasto* (debate between suitors, lovers, or husbands and wives) and the *maggio* (play of spring).[1] By genre and heritage, *le commedie rusticali* are not pastoral because they do not invite the audience into their world. Instead, as befits their predominance in the north of Italy in the sixteenth century, rustic comedies present "folk" who take themselves quite seriously while performing before a gentle, learned audience—like Bottom the Weaver and his troop, but with differences; as a result, the basic appeal lies in satire. But Sidney's adaptation of the form is elaborated. Going beyond simple *contrasti,* he introduced a pastoral motif through a singing match, which William Ringler suggests is the first in English; and he exploited a traditional topic—the active versus the contemplative life—in a debate shaped to be an appeal on behalf of Leicester for a gesture from the Queen signifying her favor.

The two extant versions—that printed at the end of the 1598 collection of Sidney's works and that recently discovered in manuscript along with a new transcription of the *Old Arcadia*[2]—are both without title and simply begin with a description of what actually took place: as the Queen was walking through a garden at Wanstead, "there came sodenly amonge the trayne one apparelled Like an honeste mans wyf of the Countrie," who, crying out for justice, is brought kneeling before Her Majesty. The plot of the entertainment—we hesitate, in spite of Stephen Orgel's recent argument, to use the term "masque"[3]—is simple enough: the woman has a daughter, whom the local folk have crowned as the Lady of the month of May, and who cannot choose between the two men who are wooing her, Espilus, a rich shepherd of "smale Desertes and no faultes," and Therion, a forester of "manie Desertes and manie faultes." But such a plot was all that Sidney needed to carry out his basic purpose: to entertain by presenting a variety of rustic types in speech, song, and dance—and to flatter the Queen by having each rustic acknowledge the majesty of Elizabeth without "knowing" that she was Her Majesty, and by leaving the choice of suitors to her. The ultimate purpose of the entertainment lies in this final choice, for the active Therion is clearly a Leicester-figure, as were Sylvanus and Deep-Desire, the speakers in Gascoigne's "farewell" at Kenilworth.

Direct as *The Lady of May* is in conception, it nevertheless reveals two aspects of Sidney's art which became more apparent as he wrote more: his ability to reveal character through speech and his refusal to see life as a series of simple oppositions. Need-less to say, Sidney did not provide the Queen with a speech or even presume to record what she said when she made her choice, but all the other "actors" are fully characterized. To begin with, the country woman who asks the Queen to prevent a fight between the suitors and their respective followers speaks in a strainedly balanced manner which is further undercut by random malaprop-isms, thus revealing her country background at a moment when she is both desperate and wishes to appear dignified.

After the country woman leaves a "Supplicacion" with the Queen—which is, in actuality, a two-stanza poem in praise of the Queen, the only one Sidney ever wrote—a group of six shepherds and one of six foresters appear, each trying to pull to its side the May Lady, while a fourteenth person, the village schoolmaster, a man "fully perswaded of his owne Learned wysdome," tries to break up the fray, "where for answer he receaved many vnlearned blowes." As soon as they see the Queen, however, all fall silent.

The first to speak is Lalus, an old shepherd whose nascent euphuism so prevents him from explaining the matter at hand that he is forced to introduce Master Rombus, the schoolmaster, who "can better disnounce the whole foundation of the matter." Rombus is a typical product of the academically oriented Northern Renaissance: the pedagogue who wallows in complicated syntax using his little Latin and less Greek to coin inkhorn terms in what he thinks is a grand display of method and learning. This type, an expected projection of a schoolboy's age-old inclination to bur-lesque his mentor, was a staple part of academic drama; and the character was carried over into popular drama (reinforced by the pedant of *commedia dell'arte*), as can be seen in Holofernes in *Love's Labour's Lost*.

Rombus's complicated comic speech in his attempt to "dis-nounce" things is finally interrupted by the May Lady, who sends him away. Then, kneeling before the Queen, she presents her case in naturally flowing phrases and easy terms, revealing her innate charm and intelligence:

Do not thincke sweete and gallante Ladie that I do abase my self this much vnto you because of your gaye apparrell, for what is so brave as the naturall beautie of the flowers nor because a certeyne gentleman heere by seekes to do you all the honor he can in his house that is not the matter he is but our neighbour and theis be our owne groves, nor yet because of your greate estate since no estate can be compared to be the ladie of the sole month of maye as I am so that since both this place and this tyme are my servantes, you maye be suer I wolde looke for reuerence at your handes yf I did not see some thinge in your face which makes my yeelde to you, the troth is you excell me in all thinges wherin I desier most to excell, and that makes me geve this homage vnto you as to the beautifullest Ladie theis woodes haue ever receaved.

As she continues, she identifies her suitors and presents her problem:

I like them both and love nether, *Espilus* is the richer but *Therion* is the Livelier, *Therion* doth me manie pleasures, and stelinge me venison out of theis Forestes and manie other such like prettie and prettier services, but with all he growes to suche Rage, as some tymes he strikes me and some tyme he Rayles at me: This shepheard *Espilus* of a mylde disposition, as his fortune hath not byn to do me greate services so hath he never donne me anie wronge, but feedinge his sheepe sittinge vnder some sweete bushe, some tymes they saie he Recordes my name in dolefull verses. Now the Question I am to aske of you fayre Ladie is whether the manie Desertes and manie faultes of *Therion* or the smale Desertes and no faultes *Espilus* be to be preferred. but before you geve your Iudgemente most excellente Ladie you shall heere what each of them can say for them selves in theire Rurall songes.

With this introduction of the pastoral singing match, and true to the Lady's description of their natures, Espilus conservatively and traditionally defends the quiet, productive life of the shepherd and invites his lady to come live with him and share his wealth; but Therion offers a free life in the forest where the only wealth will be the lady herself.

As each kneels in appeal to the Queen, their followers fall into an argument over which sang the better, an argument brought into focus by Dorcus, a shepherd, and Rixus, a forester; but the argument interrupted by the mock-directions of Rombus who, pedant-like, tries to instruct them in the forms and methods of formal argumentation. As the argument proceeds, it drifts into the conventional one of the contemplative life versus the active, but with this major difference: Dorcus's defense of an innocent world implies a stagnant life, whereas Rixus tries to show that his world has the benefits of the pastoral and more: "for ours besides the quiet part, doth both strengthen the bodie and raise of the mynde with this gallante sorte of activitie."

Finally, the May Lady interrupts to ask Queen Elizabeth again to judge "whether [of] theis tooe be moste worthie of me or whether I worthie of them, and this I will saie that in Iud[g]inge me you Iudge more then me in yt." What probably came as a surprise to few, Elizabeth chose the shepherd Espilus. Surely Leicester and Sidney were disappointed; they must have hoped to coax a nod of approval from the Queen to her Earl, still a favorite, but now in the dangerous position of secretly courting Essex's widow.

This last address to the Queen, just quoted, contains two requests: to judge not only between the suitors but to judge the Lady in judging whom "you Iudge more then me in yt," which is, of course, merely a reminder to the Queen of what must have been obvious to her: she was the Lady of the *maggio*. Naturally, she chose to ignore this second charge; and, since she chose the shepherd, Orgel and David Kalstone believe that the Queen had not been paying attention to the developing logic of the presentation which is clearly weighted in favor of Therion-Leicester. Her choice proves just the opposite; like Caesar, she knew what kind of men she wanted around her, as her consistent treatment of the Sidneys, father and son, bears witness.

To guard against the Queen's choice, Sidney had provided a final song of triumph sufficiently ambiguous to be sung by either suitor. The first of three stanzas tells of a Sylvanus, the god of forests, who sounds and acts like a shepherd; the second is about a Pan, the god of shepherds, who sounds and acts like a forester; and the third has four lines of joy and two lines of lament. Furthermore, Sidney had an "epilogue" prepared if the Queen made this "wrong" choice.

After the May Lady makes an appropriate farewell to the Queen in both versions, in the recently discovered manuscript, Rombus steps forward to address the Queen in a speech which makes clearer the fact that Leicester was seeking a favorable gesture from the Queen. But the emphasis must be on the relative— clear*er*. First of all, no one ever addressed the Queen directly without endangering his standing, as Sidney was reminded the

next year. In addition to the fact that the speech is spoken by
Rombus, a final difficulty is that, by the time the scribe had
finished copying the *Old Arcadia* and started on *The Lady of May*,
he was getting tired and anxious to finish; as a result, no one can
tell here whether or not some of Rombus's errors are intentional
or only scribal.

This much may be deduced: Rombus starts his speech with a
castigation of the "obscure barbarous *per fidem perfide*," that is,
the departing foresters, who, he says, deserve to be "vapilated"
(vapulated, thrashed), thus divorcing Leicester from Therion.
Then he turns to the Queen to present her with some round agates
which have been strung to resemble a rosary. They are a gift of
the Earl, whom he calls familiarly Master Robert, an honest and
generous man, falsely accused of Romish leanings (a rumor which,
with some justice with regard to appearances, Leicester's rivals
periodically renewed). The truth is, Rombus says, that, although
the Earl has some *"papisticorum Bedorus,"* he uses them only to
say an "Elizabeth" as many times as "theare be beades on this
stringe," which he then presents with a pseudo-legal flourish to the
Queen. In his farewell, the bad Latin is his, but the plea is obviously that of Leicester: *"me vt facias ama* that is to loue me
much better than you were wounte [wont]."

When *The Lady of May* was printed in 1598 this "epilogue"
was dropped not simply because the allusions were dated, private,
and slightly damaging to the name of Leicester, but mainly because Rombus's speech is an anticlimax. All in all, the entertainment is slight enough; the energies, however, that went into its
over-all design, its various prose styles, and its poetry seem to
have awakened Sidney's latent artistic ability and ambition.

II   Old Arcadia

If Sidney's *The Lady of May* is a bit strained and did not fulfill
its ultimate purpose, surely the opposite is true of his *Old Arcadia*.
Begun possibly in 1578, probably in 1579, and completed by the
fall of 1580, *"this idle worke,"* as Sidney calls it in the dedicatory
letter to his sister the Countess of Pembroke, was meant for a
limited audience and its aim was simply to please.[4] He states in
his letter that he started his story because his sister had requested
him to, the work being *"done in loose sheetes of paper, most of
it in your presence, the rest, by sheets, sent unto you, as fast as*

they were done" (I, 3). When he emphasizes that the whole is for her and her friends only, we can easily conjure an outdoor scene at Wilton on a summer's day with Sidney reading to an adoring circle of ladies much as Samuel Richardson was later to do. But, in spite of the fact that Richardson drew his Pamela from Sidney, the voice we hear narrating the *Old Arcadia* more nearly resembles that of Richardson's rival, Henry Fielding. Like Fielding, Sidney seems to have written not in solemnity but with a sense of fun, not cheaply and easily, but with the high seriousness of detached delight. Furthermore, he seems, as did Fielding in *Joseph Andrews,* to have felt his way as he wrote. In both cases, the results have form because of the artists' innate sensibilities; nevertheless, both works are highly experimental.

The *Old Arcadia* is a fine example of Renaissance art—unselfconsciously self-conscious. Primarily it is the traditional matter of a prose—pastoral—courtly romance treated as if it were an academic five-act comedy, as Ringler, G. K. Hunter, Walter Davis, and Richard Lanham have also stated. But, in its final form, it contains the innovation of four interludes of eclogue between the acts. Through his *tractatio,* then, Sidney makes the *Old Arcadia* his own, and his signature is even found in the shepherd Philisides. But what is finally distinctive about the *Old Arcadia* is that each Book has its own describable tone, each marked by a slight shift from light to serious, a shift which moves from the voice of the delightfully ironic, highly urbane narrator who addresses the Countess of Pembroke and her fair-lady friends in "The First Book," or "Acte," to the more neutral, serious voice which reports the debates in the last Book. The whole five Books are, to be sure, a comedy; but, in addition to being one not entirely pure, it is not entirely simple.

Although the overall nature of the work is, then, complexly experimental, Sidney knew from the beginning the story which he wanted to tell; for the seed of the whole is planted at the very beginning. As was the case with *The Lady of May,* the story is clear enough: Basilius, Duke of Arcadia, not content to govern contentedly a contented people, journeys to *"Delphos"* to discover what the future holds in store. To prevent what the oracle threatens, upon his return he decides to leave his capital and to confer the rule on a deputy, Philanax, in order to sojourn for a year in rural retreat (Book I); for the oracle has said:

Thy Elder care shall from thy carefull face
By Princely meane bee stolne, and yet not lost;
Thy Younger shall with Natures bliss embrace
An uncouth Love, whiche Nature hateth moste:
Thow with thy Wyffe adultery shalt committ,
And in thy Throne, a forreyn State shall sitt,
All this on thee this fatall yeare shall hitt. (IV, 2)

But his withdrawal, of course, leads inevitably to a fulfillment of all the he would avoid.

Although Basilius takes care to disguise his elder daughter Pamela as a shepherdess and places her in the humble home of the foolish shepherd Dametas (whose wife Miso is a shrew and whose daughter Mopsa is an imbecile), Pamela elopes (in Book III) with the *"Princely"* Musidorus, Duke of Thessaly, who, himself in disguise as a shepherd, had been taken in service by Dametas (Book I). Because they are caught (Book IV), she is *"not lost."*

As for his younger daughter Philoclea, Basilius interprets the *"uncouth Love"* as incest and is therefore not worried; but she falls unnaturally in love with a "woman" (Book I), who is actually another prince in disguise, Musidorus' cousin Pyrocles. Pyrocles had fallen immediately in love with Philoclea when he saw her picture, after he and his cousin Musidorus had been shipwrecked off the Arcadian coast and were being succored by a gentleman who told them Basilius's plan. In order to steal into the rural retreat, Pyrocles had disguised himself as the Amazon Cleophila.

In addition to Philoclea, both Basilius and his highly passionate wife Gynecia fall madly in love with Cleophila-Pyrocles at first sight, but Gynecia is not fooled by the disguise (Book I). Because Pyrocles is able to arrange an assignation in which husband and wife both think their partner will be Cleophila-Pyrocles, Basilius does indeed commit adultery with his wife (Book III).

After Basilius discovers that he has been bed-tricked (Book IV), he takes a sleep potion, thought by Gynecia to be a love potion, and falls into a trance. Because all believe that he is dead, Pyrocles's father Evarchus, King of the *"forreyn State"* of Macedonia, assumes the throne in order to restore order. After Evarchus has sentenced Gynecia to death for murder, his own son Pyrocles for attempted rape of Philoclea (in Book III), and Musidorus for abduction of a princess, Basilius awakes, and the story ends happily (Book V).

As such, the story is sufficiently interesting to divert. But what makes it thoroughly entertaining is Sidney's comic handling of his material through maintenance of narrative detachment from the action, and through an exploitation of rhetoric in such a way that word rarely answers deed. Although in both of these aspects of his art there is great variety, on the one hand, it is unconsciously so—the initial nature and role of his narrator changes during the course of the story—but, on the other hand, the variety is fully intentioned—Sidney's mastery of styles, from the burlesque of Mopsa and Dametas, through the mockery of the lovers, to the dignity of the final trial, is fully controlled.

For his structure, Sidney used, as has been indicated, the Terentian formula, as deduced by the commentators from Donatus through Willichius, for five-act comedy: protasis, beginning of the epitasis, the development of the epitasis, the highest epitasis, and the catastrophe. Act I introduces the locale and principal persons, and establishes all of the relationships necessary for the epitasis of this "very stage play of Love" (IV, 50), which in the *Old Arcadia* consists basically of two plans: that of Pyrocles to seduce Philoclea while tricking Basilius and Gynecia, and that of Musidorus to elope with Pamela while gulling Dametas, Miso, and Mopsa. Act II shows how the inroads necessary for the success of each plan are made, but in such a way that Basilius interprets the events as a favorable fulfillment of the oracle. Act III shows the seeming success of the plans, and Act IV shows their actual, disastrous results. But all is resolved in Act V, which, in keeping with the accepted formula, is highly "moral." That Sidney should turn to such a formula in an early work follows naturally from his grammar school and university education, just as does his emphasis on rhetoric and debate. But there is nothing automatic or pat about Sidney's use of rhetoric and presentation of debate; instead, as in *The Lady of May,* he uses style to reveal personality.

At the outset, the audience—the Countess of Pembroke and her friends—meets the narrator, whom we might as well call Sidney because, as in Fielding, the narrator assumes the position of an interlocutor. Although he begins abruptly, simply setting the scene in Arcadia, there is something in the voice that catches attention:

In this place some tyme there dwelte a mighty Duke named *Basilius,* a Prince of sufficient skill, to governe so quyett a Contrie, where the good myndes of the former Princes had sett downe good Lawes, and the well bringing up of the People did serve as a moste sure Bonde to keepe them: Hee marryed *Gynecia,* the Daughter of the Kinge of *Cyprus,* a Lady worthy enoughe to have had her Name in continuall Remembrance, yf her later tyme had not blotted her well governed youthe: Allthoughe the wounde fell more to her owne Conscyence, then to the knouledg of the worlde, fortune somethinge supplying her wante of vertue. (IV, 1)

Together, the qualifiers—"*some* time," "*sufficient* skill," "worthy *enough,*" "*something* supplying"—suggest a man not totally engaged with his story, one who "sees" his characters, but does no more than suggest what their surfaces are like; as the narrative progresses, the characters themselves reveal their actual dimensions. At the same time, though, the narrator maintains a genteel aloofness in the presence of the audience; after suggesting that "perchance" Basilius's wife and daughters might have been inwardly a bit jealous when they observed Basilius's obvious enchantment with "Cleophila," he goes on teasingly to say, "Yow Ladyes knowe best whether sometymes yow feele impression of that passion, for my parte, I wolde hardly thincke that the affection of a mother and the noble mynde of *Pamela* coulde bee over throwne with so base a thing as envy ys" (IV, 35). So he stands between story and audience, seeing and reporting, all in urbane irony. Not for him to get too involved; Musidorus, confessing to Pyrocles-Cleophila his love for Pamela, "began to recoumpt unto her all this I have allredy toulde you: But with suche passionate delating of yt, that, for my parte I have not a feeling Insighte enoughe into the matter, to bee able lyvely to express yt, suffyseth yt, that what so ever a possessed hart, with a good tongue to a dere frende coulde utter, was at that tyme largely sett forthe" (IV, 38).

Because of this stance, the narrator can simply report what happens and what is said, but he does so with just enough irony to keep the audience as detached as he is. After Basilius has returned from the oracle, he confides in "one chosen frende of his named *Philanax,*" who is wholly dedicated to the welfare of the Duke and Dukedom; "in suche a man had *Basilius* bene happy, yf his mynde (corrupted with a Princes fortune) had not resolved to use a frendes secretsie, rather for Confirmacion of fancyes, then correcting of errors" (IV, 3). No more than this brief observation is needed to introduce the first debate, one in which Philanax, speaking calmly and directly, points out the double folly of not taking day by day what life offers and of forsaking the obligation of rule. Basilius, nevertheless, is convinced that his plan to withdraw and turn the government over to Philanax is wise, using "muche Dukely sophistry to deceyve him self and making his will, wisdome" (IV, 6).

As soon as the Duke withdraws to the country, Pyrocles and Musidorus arrive shipwrecked in Arcadia, "and bycause this matterr ronnes principally of them, a fewe wordes, howe they came hether, will not bee superfluous" (IV, 7). In few words, then, we are told their heritage, excellence, and ages, and that they have been out in the world undertaking chivalric quests, which fully to describe "ys a worcke for a higher style then myne" (IV, 8). That work, whether or not Sidney had it presently in the back of his mind, would be the *New Arcadia;* but this work is comedy, and enough is revealed to allow the characters to act their parts.

Pyrocles does not go against the course of philosophy by merely falling in love at first sight; but he does so at first sight of a *picture.* His love establishes the basis for the second debate of the book, the familiar topic: is true virtue achieved properly through following love or reason? And the debate, as were so many schoolboy exercises and as simultaneously Lyly was doing in his *Euphues,* is made dramatic by having one pledged friend try to "save" another by full application of the colors, schemes, and tropes of rhetoric. To Musidorus, love is only a passion, a sensual outshooting of appetite; true virtue lies in "a mynde well trayned," in "Inwarde good," and in "meynteyning a right harmony." But to Pyrocles, the mind must rest or it will break; furthermore, love is stimulated by beauty and beauty leads to the Good.

All is breath-takingly argued back and forth for twenty pages, in long speeches and short; but the narrator, in describing the breaks and pauses, keeps us from taking sides so that the immediate effect is comic and entertaining; for we are not allowed to forget that what we are witnessing is a display in which two well-trained Elizabethans parry and thrust with words, exploiting all the techniques of rhetoric: "*Musidorus* had all this while helde his looke fixed uppon *Pyrocles* countenaunce and with no less loving attention, marcked, howe his wordes proceeded from him. . . . For having in the beginning of *Pyrocles* speeche (whiche defended his solitarynes) framed in his mynde a Reply ageanst yt, in the prayse of Honorable action, . . . when hee founde Pyrocles leave that, and falle to suche an affected praysing of the place, hee lefte yt likewyse, and joyned therein with him, because hee founde him in that humor, utter more store of passyon" (IV, 13).

But once Musidorus starts speaking, "*Pyrocles* mynde was all this while so fixed uppon an other Devotion, that, hee no more attentively marcked his frendes discourse, then the Chylde, that hathe leave to play, marckes the last parte of his Lesson, or the diligent Pylott in a daungerus tempest, dothe attend to the unskill-full passinger: yet the very sounde having lefte the generall poyntes of his speeche in his mynde, the respect hee bare to his frende, broughte forthe this Answer, (having first payde up his late accus-tomed tribute of Syghes)" (IV, 17–18).

There is an effect beyond the immediate, however; when we find that, in spite of his Platonic theorizing, Pyrocles is really interested in the flesh (IV, 43), and that, in spite of his Aris-totelian moralizing, Musidorus falls in love at first sight of Pamela (IV, 36–37), we realize that these are, after all, only young men of seventeen or eighteen, respectively, who know more of books than of life. The combination of the immediate and ultimate comedy proves that Sidney, far from being the slave of rhetoric, was so its master that he could exploit the lessons of his youth in delightful satire of them. If not in time, at least in technique, this Sidney is far removed from the Sidney who created Rombus.

The counterpart of Rombus in the *Old Arcadia* is the foolish shepherd Dametas, and in his creation Sidney again evinces a major advance in technique. Where Rombus only brings to mind Holofernes, Dametas is worthy of a place alongside the best of Shakespeare's low clowns. After Musidorus is won over, Pyrocles, now the Amazon "Cleophila," fully in love, breaks out into a song which wakes Dametas "oute of his sleepe (the best thinge his lyfe coulde bringe forthe)" (IV, 26). Because Dametas has been charged with the protection of the retreat, he "remembred the *Dukes* commaundement, and glad hee mighte use his authority in chyding, came swearing to the place, where *Cleophila* was, with a voyce like him, that playes *Hercules* in a play and god knowes never had *Hercules* fancy in his heade" (IV, 28). Trying to chase "her" away, he only amuses "her" inner "spirite" at a time when "she" thought "she" could only entertain sadness:

Thy spirite, (sayde Dametas) dooest thow thincke mee a Spirite? I tell thee, I am the *Dukes* officer, and have the charge of him & his Daughters. O Perle (saide sobbinge *Cleophila*) that so vyle an Oyster shoulde keepe thee? By the Combecase of *Diana*, sware *Dametas*, this woman ys madd. Oysters and Pearles? Doest thow thincke I will buy Oysters? I tell thee gett thee packing, or else I must needes bee offended. O Sunne, sayde *Cleophila*? howe long shall this Cloude live to darcken thee? and the pore Creatures that live onely by thee bee deprived of thee? These speeches to her self putt *Dametas* oute of all patience: So that hitting her upon the brest with the blunt ende of his Bill, Mayde Maryan (saide hee) am not I a person to bee answered?" (IV, 29)

The blow, of course, angers Pyrocles who sends Dametas packing by merely putting hand to sword handle: "hee went for more help to his Lodg: where knocking a good while, at lengthe hee cryed to his wyfe *Miso,* that in a whores name shee shoulde come oute to him; but in steade of that hee might heare a hollow rotten voyce, that byd him lett her alone, like a knave as hee was for shee was busy aboute my Lady *Pamela*" (IV, 29).

Miso's speech characterizes her; we would recognize her shrewish nature even if we had not been told two pages before that Dametas "had for love, chosen his wyfe, *Miso,* yet, so handsome a belldame, that shee was counted a Witche, onely for her face, and her splay foote, neyther inwardly nor owtewardly, was there any good thing in her, but, that shee observed *Decorum;* having in a wretched body a froward mynde, neither was there any humor, in which her husband and shee coulde ever agree, but in disagreeing" (IV, 27). Their daughter Mopsa is totally theirs.

When Dametas returns to the retreat, we rapidly meet the remainder of the cast of characters: after Mopsa, the voluptuous but naive Philoclea, the courtly but obtuse Basilius, the austere but strikingly handsome Gynecia, and the poised and pretty Pamela. Then, after Musidorus returns to the retreat disguised as the shepherd Dorus so that he can stay by his friend, but immediately falls in love (I, 35–36), the protasis is completed: "Fortune had framed a very stage play of Love amonge these fewe folkes" (IV, 50). A shepherd loves a princess, and she loves him; but each must hide the fact; a duke loves a man because he thinks she is a woman; a duchess loves an Amazon because she knows he is a man; and that man loves a princess, "but, sweete *Philoclea* grewe

shortly after of all other into worste Terme, for taking her to bee
suche as shee professed, desyer shee did, but shee knewe not what:
And shee longed to obteyne that, wherof shee her self coulde not
imagyn the Name, but full of unquyet imaginacyons, rested onely
unhappy, bycause shee knewe not her good happ" (IV, 50). At
the end, they all leave together to watch by torchlight some "pastoralles," some of which the narrator will report "to ease yow
fayre Ladyes of the tedyousnes of this longe discourse" (I, 51).

The entertainment had been planned for that same afternoon,
at which time all but Basilius left the retreat. But the three ladies
and two princes had no sooner arrived at the scene of the pastorals
than a lion and a bear burst forth. The shepherds ran away, Philoclea fell into Pyrocles' arms, and Pamela fainted. Lanham has
suggested that these animals are emblems of the princes under the
sway of passion; if so, they are only slightly so. Sidney makes no
comment, allows the princes to slay the beasts, and emphasizes
that the excitement is mainly provocation for love, and the nature
of the love is clear: just as Pyrocles kills the lion, Philoclea flees
and Pyrocles pursues, but not very rapidly because "her light
Nimphlyk apparell beeyng carryed up with the wynde, that,
muche of those beutyes shee woulde at an other tyme have will-
ingly hidden, were presented to the eye of the twyce wounded
Cleophila: which made *Cleophila* not followe her over hastely,
leste shee shoulde too soone deprive her self of that pleasure"
(IV, 43). This passage perfectly captures the attitude and tone
of Book I; its Elizabethan audience would *know* that the princes
were being "bad boys," but that is the simple key to the sophisticated, courtly fun.

Because the eclogues are *pastoral,* they have attitudes and tones
which contrast with those of the Books or Acts; and because they
are pastoral, serious moralizing enters the *Old Arcadia* through
them. But even in this instance, the fact that the eclogues are conventional allows them to please more than instruct. We shall consider the poetry of the eclogues in the next chapter; from the narrative point of view no "action" takes place, although the story
told by Histor of the plight of Plangus who has been sent out by
Queen Erona in search of Pyrocles and Musidorus, whom she
needs to save her, not only reveals the knightly achievements of
the princes, but also points up their present delinquency. Still, the

emphasis in the songs is on love, and, appropriately, love as yet unrequited.

After having set his stage in Book I, the narrator in Book II allows his actors to step forward without introduction to reveal themselves and, of course, to get the epitasis under way. Initially, the "action" consists only of having the principals one after another assume stage-center in order to lament their predicaments, but in such a way that the character of each is distinguished from that of the others. Gynecia, because she is wise enough to know what is proper, and passionate enough to be willing to do wrong, projects and dramatizes her situation in a long, loose apostrophe (IV, 87–88); in contrast, the orator Pyrocles, after singing a song of sorrow for reason's overthrow, addresses his lute in such a well-conceived, tightly organized manner that no room is left for passion (IV, 89). The foolish Basilius sings a song of willful self-deception which perfectly introduces his "passionate" wooing of Pyrocles (IV, 91, 108–11), and the innocent Philoclea is so aroused that she feels guilty for having previously pledged herself to chastity (IV, 93, 103–106). The two most in control of themselves are Musidorus and Pamela, but they, too, are not fully self-aware. He has the cleverness and patience to woo her by "wooing" Mopsa, and she discovers that he is a prince, which "did glad her harte with having reasonable grounde to buylde her Love uppon" (IV, 101). But the "cleverness" of his indirection is really unnecessary because poor Mopsa "was allmoste broughte asleepe with the sweete delivery of his Lamentacyons" (IV, 101), and the reasonable ground of Pamela's love does not extend far enough to include parental consultation and consent even though Musidorus has made clear his desire to elope with her.

In a parallel scene, Philoclea and Pyrocles became engaged after he identified himself, and they too do not seek parental consent, but for the better reason that both father and mother, as well as daughter, are in love with the same person. Before the Book closes, in parallel to Book I, a violent disturbance breaks out: the comic rebellion of the Phagonians, which is repulsed mainly by Pyrocles, first by arms and then by oratory. As is befitting, the pastorals which follow Book II focus on the conflict of reason and passion in love; and, as Histor's stories (ostensibly, but only tangentially, about Musidorus and Pyrocles) and Philisides's lament seem to indicate, passion rules in the extreme.

Book II is well, although rather impersonally, set forth; but the narrator returns to the stage in Book III, or at least can be seen in the wings, for here his obvious delight in his characters is more carefully sublimated within his descriptions than in Book I. Book III is devoted to the plots of Pyrocles and Musidorus, and each receives about the same attention; but the final emphasis falls on that of Pyrocles. The two princes open Book III by repledging their friendship, exchanging news, and telling plans. After they are parted by the arrival of Basilius, who is quickly dismissed, Pyrocles wanders off in pursuit of his friend only to discover a cave, into which he is enticed by a sorrowful, lamenting voice. Too late he discovers Gynecia, who starts to make violent overtures, and, just as he reluctantly tells himself that he might as well succumb, Sidney, using the first person, breaks in and shifts over to Musidorus.

In order to elope with Pamela, Musidorus must get rid of the family of Dametas, which he does by capitalizing on what he finds is the basic weakness of each: "The Muddy mynde of *Dametas* hee founde moste easily stirred with Covetusnes: The Curst myscheevous harte of *Miso* moste apte to bee tickled with Jelosy, as whose rotten brayne coulde thinck well of no body but younge Mistris *Mopsa,* who coulde open her eyes uppon no thinge that did not all to beewonder her, hee thoughte Curyosity the fittest Bayte for her" (IV, 175). As a result, he sends Dametas in a fruitless quest of buried treasure, Miso to town to prevent a non-assignation of Dametas, and Mopsa to sit in what she believes is a wishing tree; and Musidorus times the gulling of each in such a way that he and Pamela will have a whole night for their elopement.

As the two lovers set out, Pamela suffers some pangs of conscience and reminds Musidorus at some length that he has pledged to respect her virtue (shades of things to come!); he responds in a comparably elevated speech; and thus "In suche delighttfull Discourses kept they on theyre Journey mevntayning theyre hartes in that right Harmony of affection, whiche dothe enterchaungeably deliver eche unto other, the secrett worcking of theyre Sowles" until Pamela tires and they stop in a pine grove (IV, 186). The delightful setting elicits songs from each, and Musidorus sets forth a bountful repast, the combination of which lulls Pamela to sleep. As Musidorus bends over her, examining the beauty of her face, his inward thoughts praise each feature through the standard clichés of the Provençal-Petrarchan catalogue, one ending with her mouth. But the lips and breath excite him to begin to forget his pledge and to seek a kiss. Because of the exalted mock-romantic style of this passage, critics have fallen into the trap of thinking that Musidorus seeks to rape Pamela; hence, I quote the passage in full:

Hee was compeld to putt his face as Lowe to hers as hee coulde, sucking the Breathe with somuche Joy, that hee did determeyn in hym self there had bene no Lyfe, to a Camelyons yf hee mighte bee suffred to enjoy that foode. But eche of these having in his harte a severall worcking all joynde together did so drawe his will into the nature of theyre Confederacy, that now his promyse began to have but a faynting force, and eche thoughte that rose ageanst those desyers was receyved but as a Straunger to his Counseyll, well experyencing in hym self, that no vowe ys so stronge as the avoyding of occasions: So that rysing softely from her overmastered with the fury of delighte (having all his Sences parciall ageanst hym self, and enclyned to his wellbeloved Adversary) hee was bent to take the vauntage of the weykenes of the watche, and see whether at that season hee coulde wynn the Bullwarck before tymely help mighte come. And now hee began to make his aproches when to the just punishment of his broken promyse, and moste unfortuned barr of his longe pursued & atcheeved desyers, there came by a Doszen Clownish villeynes armed with dyvers sortes of weapons. (IV, 190)

The only way to understand this passage is to remember that it is meant for the Countess and the fair ladies of her circle; therefore, it is designed both to titillate and to tease. Because the passage is suggestive and open to misinterpretation, when Sidney discovered that his *Old Arcadia* was receiving a wider circulation than he intended, he drew up notes for its amendment; namely, the suppression of the second half of the passage just quoted and a toning down of the conclusion of Book III, Pyrocles's assignation with Philoclea.

Sidney returns to Pyrocles in the same manner that he left him, simply switching abruptly from Musidorus in straits to Pyrocles in the clutches of Gynecia, who, after a long pleading speech, "(under a fayned Rage tearing her Cloathes) . . . discovered some partes of her fayre body, which yf *Cleophilas* hart had not beene so fully posset . . . no doubt yt woulde have yeelded to that gal-launt assaulte" (IV, 193–94). Then follows a wonderful ration-alization: Pyrocles, a true gentleman, who remembers that he must "wade betwixt Constancy and Curtesy," embraces Gynecia and kisses her "once or twyce"!

With this same spirit of detached delight Sidney presents the assignation of Pyrocles and Philoclea, which climaxes the high comedy of the work (just as the opening of Book IV climaxes the low). Because both lovers are noble yet young, they are simul-taneously and confusedly idealistic and sensuous, which, of course, permits Sidney and the audience to be aloof from them. For exam-ple, the dully, slowly evolved plan of Pyrocles to delude the parents into adultery and the extreme self-pity of Philoclea who is love-sick in bed are neither suspenseful nor sad, but are amus-ing; for the reader knows full well the details of the prophecy (IV, 195–210). On the other hand, Sidney the author remains close enough to all his characters to present them in their fullness; he shows, for example, the subtle psychological effects of illicit desire in Gynecia as she dresses (rather undresses) and departs for the cave (IV, 211–12), and the broader self-delusion, rein-forced by physical clumsiness, of Basilius who, it is suggested, falls asleep when he is finally arrived in the position which will, he thinks, allow him to satisfy his desire (I, 212–15).

When the focus finally shifts entirely to the lovers, the attitude and tone turn completely Ovidian, Pyrocles acting and talking like Shakespeare's Venus and Marlowe's Leander, while Philoclea is a forerunner of Adonis and Hero. This intellectual comedy of the flesh is capped by the introduction of the long, sensual cata-logue-song which passes through Pyrocles' mind as he comes to the bed of the nearly naked Philoclea. That Sidney made more expansions and revisions in this poem, as Ringler has shown, than in any other is proof positive that he was no "puritan," and the fashion in which he follows its conclusion shows how masterfully he controls his authorial stance:

But doo not thincke (Fayre Ladyes) his thoughtes had suche Leysure as to ronne over so longe a Ditty: The onely generall fancy of yt came into his mynde fixed uppon the sence of the sweet Subject. Where using the benefitt of the Tyme, and fortifying hym self, with the Confessing her late faulte, (to make her nowe the sooner yeelde to penance) turning the passed greeffes and unkyndenes, to the excess of all kynde Joyes (as passyon ys apte to slyde into all Contrary) beginning nowe to envy *Argus* thowsand eyes *Brierius* hundred handes, feighting ageanst a Weyke resistance whiche did stryve to bee overcome; Hee gives mee occasyon to leave hym in so happy a plighte, least my Penn mighte seeme to grudge, at the due Blisse of these pore Lovers, whose Loyalty had but smalle respite of theyre fyery Agonyes. And nowe *Lalus* pype dothe come to my hearing, whiche invites mee to his Mariage that in this Season was celebrated betweene hym & the handsome *Kala,* whom longe hee had loved: whiche, I hope (Fayre Ladyes) youre eares bee not so full of great matters, that yow will dislayne to heare. (IV, 226–27)

When the eclogues after Book III turn out to be a full celebration of marital love, the irony of this last line is made explicit. Books I and II each ended with a disordering outbreak, but Book III seemingly ends in smoothness. Only the counterpoint of the pastoral tribute to the logic and order of marriage suggests otherwise, and one consciously ironic passage ties Book III and the eclogues together: "Thus constantly continewying, thoughe hee [Lalus] were none of the fayrest, at lengthe hee wann *Kalas* harte, the honestest wenche in all those quarters: And so with Consent of bothe Parentes (withoute which neyther *Lalus* woulde aske, nor *Kala* graunte), Theyre Mariage day was appoynted, whiche because yt fell oute in this tyme, I thincke yt shall not bee Impartinent to remember a litle oure Shepeheardes, while the other greater persons are eyther sleeping or otherwyse occupyed" (IV, 228).

The juxtaposition of the urbane, sophisticated comedy of Book III and the warm, humble human comedy of the Third Eclogues complicates the developing tone of the *Old Arcadia,* a tone which in Book IV, more so than previously, is a mixture of laughable and serious, sometimes together in mock-heroic, more often in separation, and at the very beginning either one or the other:

The Everlasting Justice (using oure selves to bee the punisshers of oure faultes, and making oure owne actions the beginninge of oure Chastisement, that oure shame may bee the more manifest, and oure Repentance followe the sooner,) tooke *Dametas* at this present (by whose folly the others wysdome mighte receyve the greater overthrowe) to bee the instrument of reveyling the secrettst Connyng:

So evill a grounde dothe evell stande uppon, and so manifest yt ys, that no thing Remaynes strongly, but that whiche hathe the good foundacyon of goodnes. (IV, 247)

If the name of Dametas did not occur here, we might feel that Sidney was preparing for the disclosure of the high point of the epitasis, the low fortunes of all, noble and humble, which in keeping with the Terentian scheme, must be handled morally. But Dametas's name does occur, and the passage in fact introduces the most evenly sustained passage of comic narration in the work: Dametas returns, disappointed of his treasure, to find that Pamela has escaped; that Mopsa, in the tree, thinks he is Apollo; and that Miso, on her return, is ready to flay him (IV, 247–54). His main concern, of course, is to find Pamela because his life depends on doing so. Rushing to Philoclea's room in search of her sister, he finds Pyrocles instead; and he realizes that *this* information might bate the King's fury, but, when he is told by shepherds that the King is dead, he is, naturally, happy to be relieved of the burden of his guilt!

The structural method of Book IV is initiated at this point when a flashback to Basilius and Gynecia in the cave relates their story up to the present moment: how the Duke had passed the night "more happy in Contemplacyon then action, (having had his spirites sublimed with the sweete Imagination of embracing the moste desyered *Cleophila*)" (IV, 255–56); how in the morning he had joyfully pondered the question "O who woulde have thoughte there coulde have bene suche difference betwixt women?" (IV, 256); how Gynecia had revealed herself; and how he, humbled, had asked forgiveness and, in his distraction, had drunk the sleep potion. After he has "died," the flashback continues with the focus on Gynecia. Her pangs of conscience are great indeed, and would be moving were it not discovered that she is moved more by the temporary loss of Pyrocles's love than by the permanent one of her husband. But she has sufficient pride and character to "confess" to the shepherds when they discover her crying over her husband's body. Because of the enormity of the event and its political implications, the tone is mixed, and the lamentations of the shepherds are sincere (IV, 263–66).

This note of sincerity is reinforced when Philanax, having heard about the Phagonian rebellion (Book II), arrives to visit his Duke and adds his noble, politically oriented lament to theirs (IV, 267–68). He soon takes charge; he arrests Gynecia and orders all to the house; and, at this point we get our second flashback, now to Pyrocles and Pamela.

As soon as Dametas had left the room, Pyrocles had awakened, "or rather as I thincke that hee had but litle slept that Nighte, so, the sweete embracement hee enjoyed gave his sences a very easy salve to come to them selves" (IV, 269). And "embracement," in spite of the dirty minds of generations of readers, is the right word; for these young lovers have done only what young lovers have always longed to do: spent the night in each other's arms without indulging in the pleasure of intercourse. The fact, however, is unimportant because Dametas thinks and reports the worst, which Pyrocles overhears; and he immediately realizes the ironic situation they are in: they will be condemned to death because such is the fate of those "founde in acte of Mariage withoute solempnity of Mariage" (IV, 270). That Philoclea still has an "Innocent sowle" does not matter (IV, 270), for "the weyke judgment of Man woulde condempne that as a deathe deserving vice in her, whiche had in truthe never broken the bandes of a true Living vertue. And howe often his eye turned to his attractive *Adamant,* so often did an unspeakeable horror stryke his noble harte to Consyder so unrype yeares, so faultles a Beuty, the Mansyon of so pure goodnes shoulde have her youthe so untymely Cutt of, her naturall perfections unnaturally consumed her vertue rewarded with shame" (IV, 271).

When Pyrocles decides that he can save her good name by committing suicide, Sidney does not handle the situation with pathos but with humor, for Pyrocles's attempt to impale himself on the window bar serves only to wake Philoclea and to give occasion for an extended, high-style, mock-romantic debate on the subject of suicide. Pyrocles, "not so muche perswaded as delighted by her well conceyved and sweetly pronounced speeches," agrees to live because she threatens that she will follow him in death if he insists upon suicide (IV, 278). While the treatment is comic, the subject and the lovers are serious; when Philanax enters to arrest them, the treatment, too, becomes serious; but it remains so only until the sudden return to Musidorus and Pamela who have been captured and brought back to the retreat.

When Sidney returns to Musidorus and Pamela, he again adopts

his mocking, hyperbolic manner as he describes in a third flashback how the "Remnaunte of those *Phagonian* Rebells" interrupted Musidorus as he bent over Pamela ready to kiss her and
how he fought them (IV, 286). But once they seize Pamela, forcing Musidoras to drop his sword, the tone again becomes serious,
and remains so for the balance of the *Old Arcadia.* Indeed, the
conversation on chance between the lovers has a dignity of matter
that is reinforced by rhythms that call to mind the Prayer Book
(IV, 290–92).

In keeping with the established pattern, Book IV ends with a
tumult, or outbreak. With Basilius "dead," Arcadia is without a
ruler, thus affording Sidney the opportunity to describe at length
the resultant civil discord and strife. In this passage we can see
Sidney the courtier, fully desirous of a strong monarchy, and Sidney the Elizabethan, fully afraid of disorder. But the artist is in
control so that the tense efforts of Philanax, the rivalries among
nobles, and the dissidence of Tymantus are vividly, but objectively
described. The whole passage serves as a serious counterweight to
the sustained comic narrative which opened Book IV.

Because the attitude has turned political, and the tone serious,
by the end of Book IV, the Fourth Eclogues fittingly show the
shepherds withdrawn to a far hill where they simply and movingly
lament the death of Basilius; and their lack of ambition acts as a
counter-theme to the political turmoil that reigns below among the
nobles. Histor tells no stories of the princes, for they are now fully
in the center of the action (even though disguised now by a second
pair of assumed names): Pyrocles is charged with the rape of
Philoclea and with being in league with Gynecia; Musidorus, with
treason for having abducted the heir apparent and with possibly
being in league with Gynecia and Pyrocles.

Book V opens with the fortuitous arrival in Arcadia of King
Evarchus of Macedonia (Pyrocles's father), whom Philanax per-
suades to assume the throne in order to try the prisoners and
restore peace in the land. Because the focus is on ideas and judg-
ments, the emphasis is, as it was in Book I, on rhetoric. But in
Book V all is serious, and the speeches are presented without
the controlling asides of the narrator. In fact, in the passages of
narration which link the various speeches and deliberations, Sidney writes in the balanced, restrained periods which the world has
come to call the "Arcadian" style: *"Evarchus* did not further

exceede his meanest Subject with the greatnes of his fortune, then hee did surmount the greatnes of his fortune, with the greatnes of his mynde. In somuche that those thinges which often tymes the best sorte thinck rewardes of Vertue, hee helde them not at so hye a pryce, but esteemed them Servauntes to well dooyng: The Reward of vertue beeyng in yt self, on which his Inward love was so fixed, that never was yt dissolved into other desyers, but keeping his thoughtes true to them selves, was neither beguyled with the paynted glasse of pleasure, nor dazeled with the false lighte of Ambition" (IV, 331). In Book V we can sense that Sidney is ready to begin the *New Arcadia.*

In order to prepare for the trial proper, Sidney gives in short but precise passages descriptions of the various states of mind of the prisoners: Gynecia, the sisters, and finally the princes (IV, 340–44). When he comes to these latter, we are afforded the excellent opportunity to measure the degree of change in technique which has taken place since Book I because of a second debate on love and friendship. Here, however, there is no comic self-delusion; rather, we find a subtle sense of self-awareness (IV, 344–46).

The trial scene is presented in full dress; all the pomp and ceremony which the Elizabethans loved is there in plenty; but, as in life, the ceremony is not an end in itself. Evarchus "well knewe" that "in these pompous Ceremonyes . . . a Secrett of government" did much consist (IV, 348). Evarchus is all in black in the seat of judgment, and he is surrounded in appropriate order by the nobles and people. The *"Dukes* body beeyng layde uppon a Table just before *Evarchus,* and all covered over with black, the Prisoners namely the *Duchess* and twoo younge *Princes* were sent for to appeare in the Protectors name: whiche name was the Cause they came not to knowledg howe nere a Kinseman was to judge of them, but thought hym to bee some Noble Man chosen by the Contry in this extremity" (IV, 349).

The appearance of each, down to the last detail of clothing, is described fully; and the response of the crowd is opposite to its expectation: Gynecia arouses pity because of her humility and distraction; the princes, in spite of the fact that they were "hated as Straungers," suggest forcefully "Magnanimity" and "extraordenary vertue" (IV, 350). As he enters last, Musidorus speaks out passionately "to moove the people to tender *Pamelas* fortune" and

is relieved to find that she is safe and that Arcadia is to have a pro-
tector until she reaches twenty-one (IV, 351–52). Pyrocles then
speaks in behalf of Philoclea, but, in spite of the favorable response of the crowd, Evarchus, "neither regarding a Prisoners
passionate prayer nor bearing over plausible eares to a many
headed motion" (IV, 353), pronounces that she must live with
and "like the *Vestall* Nunnes" the rest of her life. Pyrocles's reaction to the sentence should not be lost in the sweep of ceremony: "Althoughe this were a great prejudicating of *Pyrocles*
Case, yet was hee exceedingly Joyous of yt beeyng assured of his
Ladyes lyfe, and in the Depthe of his mynde not sory, that what
ende soever hee had none shoulde obtayne the after enjoying that
Jewell whereon hee had sett his Lyves happynes" (IV, 354).

Philanax, in the role of prosecutor, decides to open against
Gynecia; but "as hee was entering into his invective oration,"
she fully and openly confesses her crime, and is sentenced to be
buried alive with her husband (IV, 354–56). Philanax, formerly
prevented from displaying his invective against Gynecia, is now
ready to do so when the time comes to charge the princes. Assuming an ethos of righteous indignation, he masterfully presents his
well-ordered cases behind masks of contempt and sarcasm, passion and outrage. Although all is talk, Sidney creates drama, for
each of the princes is fully able to defend himself. Because
Philanax has passionately put forth "so cunning a Confusion, as
having mingled truthes with falshoodes, surmyses with certeyntyes,
Causes of no moment with matters capitall, scolding with com-
playning" (IV, 364), Pyrocles remains calm and relies on factual
truth.

His success in debate is indicated by the reaction of Philanax
in his accusation of Musidorus: "*Philanax* nothing the mylder for
Pyrocles purging hym self, (but rather according to the nature
of arguinge, especially when yt ys bitter) so muche the more
vehement, entered thus into his speeche ageanst *Musidorus:* Beeing so overgon with rage, that hee forgatt in his oration his precyse
Methode of Oratory" (IV, 371). As a result, Musidorus is able
to couch his defense in sarcasm directed against this "vyle Pick-
thanck," this "Master Orator," this "Brabler," this "Gentleman
[who] thinkes to wynn the reputation of a gallant speaker (by
leaving nothing unsayde which a filthy mowthe can imagyn)" (IV,
373–75).

All is so well and forcefully presented that the crowd is swayed
back and forth, but not Evarchus, who let "pass the flowers of
Rethorique" and who marked only the course of logic. After the
testimony (unrecorded, for it surely would have destroyed the
serious tone of the trial) of Dametas, Miso, and Mopsa, Philanax
rests the joint case. As Evarchus weighs the evidence, he lays the
ground for his decision with a discussion of the "Lawes of Nature
and Nations," using language and ideas which Hector later used
in Shakespeare's *Troilus and Cressida* (IV, 376–77). After re-
viewing the charges and defenses, he concludes: "That *Tymo-
phirus* [Pyrocles] shall bee throwne of, from a hye Tower, to
receyve his deathe by his Falle, *Palladius* [Musidorus] shall bee
beheaded, the tyme before the Sunne sett, the place in *Mantinea,*
the executioner *Dametas* which office hee shalle execute all the
dayes of his lyfe, for his beastly forgetting the carefull Duty owed
to his Charge" (IV, 380).

Before the sentences can be initiated, a stranger arrives who
identifies the two princes. Because of their widespread fame, all
rejoice; even "*Philanax* revengefull hart was mollifyed, when hee
sawe how from dyvers partes of the worlde so nere kinsemen
shoulde meete in suche a necessity: And withall the fame of
Pyrocles and *Musidorus* greatly drewe hym to a compassionate
Conceypte, and had all redy uncloathed his face of all shewe of
mallice" (IV, 382). But Evarchus, true king and judge, makes the
sentences stick, painful though doing so is to him. Pyrocles and
Musidorus, true princes and friends, accept their individual fates
but each pleads that the other be spared. As passion and pity
mount, Basilius awakes from his deep sleep, so that all ends in joy
and happiness:

But the solempnityes of the Marriages with the *Arcadian* pastoralles
full of many *Comicall* adventures happening to those Rurall Lovers
the straunge story of the fayre Queene *Artaxia* of *Persia* and *Erona*
of *Lydia,* with the Prince *Plangus* wonderfull Chaunces whome the
later had sent to *Pyrocles,* and the extreme affection *Amasis* kinge of
Egipt bare unto the former: The Sheperdish Loves of *Menalcas* with
Kalodulus Daughter, and the pore hopes of *Philisides* in the pursuite
of his affections, the strange Countenance of *Claius* and *Strephons*
desyer, Lastly the Sonne of *Pyrocles* and *Melidura* the fayre Daughter
of *Pamela* by *Musidorus:* who even at theyre byrthe entred into

admirable Fortunes may awake some other Spirite to exercyse his penn in that, wherewith myne ys allredy dulled. (IV, 389)

I have quoted the ending in full for two reasons: first, Sidney may here indicate the possibility of a sequel, a return to Arcadia; but he does not indicate that he had in mind a revision and expansion of the present work. Second, and more germane, is the fact that the *Arcadia* ends as it began, with the urbane and smiling voice of the narrator. In between occur the high comedy of love and the low comedy of farce, along with a display of oratorical rhetoric ranging from mock to serious; and all is framed and ultimately controlled by the bemused, detached narrator. The suggested sequel would have to be a continuation in comedy, but the actual revision is heroic, and the narrator disappears.

CHAPTER 4

Experiments in Poetry

SIDNEY'S attitude in the late 1570s toward English poetry is delightfully caught in an early poem in the *Old Arcadia*. When the time comes to introduce Mopsa, the narrator demurs "because shee bare the Sexe of a Woman," and he quotes a poem by one Alethes, "an honest man of that tyme":

What length of verse can serve brave *Mopsa's* good to show,
Whose vertues strange, and beuties such, as no man them may know?
Thus shrewdly burdned then, how can my Muse escape?
The gods must help, and pretious things must serve to shew her shape.
    Like great god *Saturn* faire, and like faire *Venus* chaste:
As smooth as *Pan,* as *Juno* milde, like goddesse *Isis* faste.
With *Cupid* she fore-sees, and goes god *Vulcan's* pace:
And for a tast of all these gifts, she borowes *Momus'* grace.
    Her forhead jacinth like, her cheekes of opall hue,
Her twinkling eies bedeckt with pearle, her lips of Saphir blew:
Her haire pure Crapal-stone; her mouth O heavenly wyde;
Her skin like burnisht gold, her hands like silver ure untryde.
    As for those parts unknowne, which hidden sure are best:
Happie be they which well beleeve, and never seeke the rest.
                                                        (Ringler, 12)

Several things are apparent. That the poem is a sonnet in praise of a woman shows Sidney's awareness of Petrarchism. The invocation of a muse and reference to the gods show Classical orientation, as does the first set of similes. The second set then shows awareness of a descriptive tradition that goes back through Provençal poetry to the Song of Songs. But the nature of these similes betrays a tendency we have already noted in Sidney, which is so typical of his age: the mocking of pedagogy. But this aspect of the poem taken together with the meter—poulters—shows Sidney's full awareness of the native poetry of his day, a poetry indebted equally to the schools and to Tottel's *Songes and Sonettes.*

I   *The Sixteenth-Century Setting*

The grand aim of pedagogues and poets for most of the sixteenth century was to discover the means of ordering the vernacular so that poetry could be achieved. To the pedagogue, such was possible because of the example of Virgil; and, because of Virgil, such was necessary if the vulgar tongue was ever to be civilized. To the poet, such ordering was possible because of the example of Chaucer, but Chaucer's meter seemed a mystery. From our point of view, we recognize, even as Dryden did not, the metrical basis of Chaucer's poetry; but the Chaucer available through Caxton and later printers was a Chaucer far removed from the one of 1400. Lacking historical perspective, successive redactors of Chaucer had silently and unconsciously kept him "up to date" during the fifteenth century while Middle English was dramatically evolving into the modern idiom. As a result, especially of the loss of French traces, Chaucer's syllabification was grossly distorted; and the pentametric line was lost. But the genius of theme and wit were obvious: because of his "matter," Chaucer was justly crowned the father of English poetry. Some, mainly Stephen Hawes, Alexander Barclay, and John Skelton, seem therefore consciously to have taken what they thought to be the intentional metrical roughness of Chaucer as a dignifying precedent, just as Spenser was to do in 1579.

To mention Skelton is to recall that the earliest meter in English was accentual, and Josephine Miles (*Eras & Modes in English Poetry*) attributes to Skelton the resurrection of the ancient two-beat, caesura, two-beat line of Old English poetry, a line which Northrup Frye claims in *Anatomy of Criticism* never had and still has not disappeared from English poetry. But the Norman conquest had softened and sophisticated English to the point that accent alone did not offer sufficient control in poetry that attempted lines more elaborate in length and more sophisticated in thought than had the simple native lyric.

The simple English lyric from the Middle Ages on is accentual syllabic. That is, it has beat running regularly through measured lines. John Gower, more at home in Latin and French, could exploit this fact of vernacular poetry, attaining and maintaining a thoroughly controlled iambic tetrameter throughout his *Confessio Amantis*. But only Chaucer attained iambic pentameter, and except for Lydgate, no one else, until Wyatt, could maintain it. There is no need, nor is there space, to rehearse the achievement of Sir Thomas Wyatt. Suffice it to say that, when he began writing, there was no defined English poetic. The only true verse being written was the native lyric; but, because it *was* native, no one would call it verse. The only poetry worthy that name was Latin—the carefully constructed Latin of Virgil, Horace, and Ovid, a Latin carefully being restored by the academic Humanists. Roger Ascham spoke for the academic majority when he praised Virgil and Horace "who by right *Imitation* of the perfit Grecians . . . brought Poetrie to perfitnesse also in the Latin tong." He wished "that we Englishmen likewise would acknowledge and understand rightfully our rude beggerly ryming, brought first into Italie by *Gothes* and *Hunnes* whan all good verses and all good learning to, were destroyd by them: and after caryed into France and Germanie and at last receyved into England by men of excellent wit."[1] In spite of Ascham's prejudice, the only possible rival to Classical Latin poetry was the vernacular Italian of Dante and Petrarch, who, unlike Chaucer, had disciples in the fifteenth century capable of establishing and developing what they had pioneered. In France, the members of the Pléiade were soon to match the achievement of the Italians by learning how to frame their native words in order to make music—to achieve the harmony, balance, and pull of poetry.

In the face of this formidable triple example, the academic Humanists in sixteenth-century England fell into despair, while the active poets from Wyatt on went about their business. What the academics wanted, of course, was a heroic line, without which no native epic could be written, without which the tongue and nation would remain "barbaric." All the poets wanted to do was sing; and they, not the theoreticians, made the essential discoveries.

Wyatt's mastery of the native lyric is proof of his genius, but his willingness and ability to learn from Petrarch and, indirectly, from Dante is proof of his talent. Immersing himself in the syllabic basis of their lines he, literally, pushed the English line back out to five feet. To be sure, much of his pentameter cannot be scanned, but this is simply one way of saying that Wyatt never lost touch with

the accentual strength of English. But, by the time of his translations of the Penitential Psalms and his three satires all in iambic
pentameter terza rima, he fully defined for the future that the
English poetry which moves and delights is accentual *and* syllabic,
the iamb being the most natural foot, and pentameter, the most
dignified length.

We do not need Surrey's moving tribute to Wyatt to recognize
his debt; the evidence is in his poetry. Surrey regularized vernacular poetry in terms of accent and syllable count, and such was his
achievement that, from the time of his death until the poetry of
Gascoigne and Sidney, absolute regularity of accent and syllable
was to be the norm of vernacular poetry. The evidence is abundant
in the simultaneous success and successive editions of Baldwin's
A Mirror for Magistrates and Tottel's *Songes and Sonettes.*

From the historical point of view, Surrey's one true innovation
went almost unnoticed: his translation of Virgil in a "straunge
meter," a meter to be called by the Elizabethans "blank verse,"
and finally one hundred years later by Milton, "the heroic line."
This innovation was practically ignored—before Marlowe, only
a few, mainly Thomas Sackville, Thomas Norton, and Gascoigne,
were bold enough to rely on accent and number alone to carry
the thrust of poetry[2]—because poets generally felt, to use Sidney's
phrase, that the "chiefe life" of vernacular poetry "standeth in that
like sounding of words, which we call Rime" (III, 44). The heritage here of Medieval Latin is clear enough, a heritage intensified
in England because of the alliterative poetry of Middle English.
And precisely because rime grew in part from decadent Latin, the
academic Humanists strove all the harder to fight against the
natural tendencies of vernacular poets.

But, if Surrey was out of step with fellow poets in scrapping
rime, he was at one with both poets and academics in translating
Virgil; for, with the Humanist revival, Virgil, along with Cicero,
became a central figure in education; he simply was the poet,
moralist, and encyclopedist par excellence. To use him as the
foundation of the search for an English heroic line, then, was
natural. Even though all schoolboys "englished" Virgil as a matter
of routine exercise, the first published translation was that of
Surrey in 1554, to be followed the next year by Thomas Phaer's,
written in fourteener couplets—a verse form which, if our ear does
not reject, our eye does if only because C. S. Lewis said it should.

But what Lewis forgot is the predominance of the ideal of regularity in the 1550s (Tottel's editor had to "correct" Wyatt), the rediscovery of the pentametric line, and the eager search for a heroic line. What would follow more logically than: if one could reach out successfully through five feet, why not six, especially in view of Latin and French epic poetry; why not six's and seven's; and then why not even all seven's? (Americans are said to get their bigger-means-better attitude from their Elizabethan ancestors.) Why not, indeed? Because the natural rhythms of the language cannot usually be sustained over such a length of meter, only occasionally so, as the first *Astrophel and Stella* sonnet proves, and as does the success of Drayton in *Poly Albion* and in other of his longer poems. But even Spenser had to pad from time to time to get a hexameter conclusion to some stanzas of *The Fairie Queene.* Furthermore, poulters and fourteeners tend to break down into the natural units of ballad measure. In fact, fourteeners were often printed as threes and fours; and, when a poet used internal rhyme, the natural break of the line was further emphasized. Some, especially Gascoigne in a few poems and Richard Edwards in the masterful *Amantium Irae,* capitalized upon the ballad-like fact of fourteeners to build sophisticated lyrics. But, for the most part, poets wrote fourteeners because they had the sanction of such examples as Phaer and because fourteeners were easy to write.

A reinforcing phenomenon of the 1560s and 1570s was the fact that poetry had a popular market, as Baldwin and Tottel discovered and as others were quick to exploit. Before this outburst, poetry was being written, but in the schools as academic exercises and in polite circles as genteel ones. But, when poetry had commercial value, some of these private endeavors were made public. A few, such as Barnabe Googe, hesitatingly "allowed" their poetry to be published; but most, even poets so diverse as Thomas Tusser and Gascoigne, frankly accepted the sudden publicity of poetry. The Earl of Oxford even contributed to printed collections, much to the amusement of Sidney, as has been noted already. Surveying the scene in the late 1570s, Sidney would have exclaimed, along with Richard Stanyhurst, "Good God what a frye of such *wooden rhythmours* dooth swarme in stationers shops."[3]

But this outburst in 1582 occurs in the preface to a work that is at the opposite extreme of the regimented rhythmers—Stanyhurst's quantitative translation of the *Aeneid,* a work which Sidney might well have encouraged; for in the late 1570s, appalled by the tendencies of native verse, he joined in study with the academic Humanists, finding himself at this time the center of a group of poets and theorists concerned with the fate of native poetry. Whether or not Sidney ever headed an English Academy—the *Areopagus* of Spenser's letter to Harvey—is beside the point. It is quite obvious that the poets of England were concerned with the development of vernacular poetry and were actively thrashing around for metrical principles by which to frame their verse, and it was quite natural for them to try to borrow the regal apparel of Latin and to exchange their ideas one with another.

Indeed, as we have noted, England was sufficiently small for people of like interests to get together or certainly to be well aware of what others were doing. And all the evidence indicates that 1579 might accurately be compared to 1922 as a pivotal year in the world of English letters. The year opened with the reception of *Euphues,* closed with the publication of *The Shepheardes Calender,* and in the midst saw the publication of Gosson's *The School of Abuse,* dedicated to Sidney at a time when he himself was actively engaged in writing and talking with friends about literature.

The actual dating of Sidney's poetry is difficult, but general deductions are possible. The year before 1579 Sidney had written his first "public" work, *The Lady of May,* which seems to have stimulated his active interest in literature. He surely had written poetry before the spring of 1578, but the three poems which appear in the entertainment, although sound and functional, are not exceptional. Between the spring of 1578 and the fall of 1580 he completed the *Old Arcadia,* which contains fifty poems, and the four interludes of eclogue, which, in turn, contain the twenty-seven poems that constitute the first extended pastoral in English. During these years Sidney intensely analyzed the nature of English poetry on his own and with friends, as can be determined by Sidney's collection called *Certaine Sonets,* which contains thirty-two poems, all but two of which Ringler believes were written before 1581. Ringler also has proved that these two, the first in the collection, were written before *Astrophel and Stella,* which I believe was started in 1581, but which he places entirely in 1582. Beside the seven poems which Ringler has collected as "Other

Poems," the only other collection by Sidney is his translation of the first forty-three Psalms, the remaining being done by the Countess of Pembroke some time after her brother's death. Of the "Other Poems," five were included in the *New Arcadia* (but only two appear to have been written specifically for that partial redaction of the *Old,* a project which had been dropped by 1584), and the last two poems are pastoral lyrics which cannot be dated because they appear only in the 1602 *A Poetical Rapsody.*

No date for Sidney's translations of the Psalms has been established. Theodore Spencer, on the basis of his evaluation of their style and poetic worth, would place them first among Sidney's literary efforts. Ringler, on the basis of source study, would place them at least in 1580; and, on the basis of what he feels is their poetic virtuosity, he would place them among Sidney's last living efforts. J. C. A. Rathmell, the latest editor of the "Sydnean Psalmes" (as John Donne called the completed work), however, places them before *Astrophel and Stella* on the basis of style. Whether they were written before 1579 or after, they are best understood in the context of Sidney's experimental poetry, poetry written in conjunction with his proclamation with Dyer of "a generall surceasing and silence of bald Rymers," as Spenser facetiously wrote to Harvey in October 1579 from Leicester House.[4]

II *The Psalms*

Ringler suggests that Sidney never finished his translation, or paraphrases, of the Psalms because he was called to the Netherlands; I suggest that he quit because he realized that this particular attempt to reform vernacular poetry was not worth the effort. Putting the Psalms into English was, of course, more than merely a poetic exercise; it was in keeping with one of the central issues of the Reformation, the movement to the use of the vernacular in Protestant churches. Before the reign of Edward, there had been constantly increasing publication of partial and whole translations of the Bible, but only hesitating use of the vernacular in churches. With the adoption of the Prayer Book in 1549, however, there was a sudden burst of translations, especially of English Psalters. In 1547, for example, Edward White had published without much flourish nineteen Psalms put into "English metre" by Thomas Sternhold; but, in 1549, he issued a collection expanded to thirty-six and, later in the year, another book augmented by eight of John Hopkins's translations. Each book contained a long dedicatory epistle to the King to explain that the main purpose of these metrical Psalms was to enable the unlearned to quickly memorize them and sing them in church. So successful was White's work that he continued issuing "Sternhold and Hopkins" augmented with the works of others so that by 1562 he had assembled all one hundred and fifty; and, in the same year, the complete collection was officially adopted for use in the Anglican Church. (For the next one hundred years hardly one year passed without a reprint of this work.) As a result, as Ringler observes, there can be no doubt that Sidney was fully aware of these Psalms; and the fact that they were in absolutely regular fourteeners must have appalled him.

The impulse to translate the Psalms was more complex than a simple esthetic reaction to "bald Rymers," for Sidney's high respect for the Psalms is clearly set forth in the *Defence*. Yet, although his manner of procedure shows Sidney consciously departing from native practice, he unconsciously is true to it; for his forty-three Psalms, except for five vaguely trochaic poems, are as absolutely regular as are Sternhold's and Hopkins's. But Sidney did not use a single meterical form throughout; rather, he followed a Continental tradition of employing a different stanza pattern in each of his poems, only two of which can be labeled: Psalm 30 in terza rima, and 19 in broken fourteener couplets.

Because of the similarity of form of the two versions of Psalm 19, they illustrate how Sidney moved away from Sternhold. The first two stanzas of Sternhold's version have the forward thrusting, thumping regularity familiar in hymns such as "A Mighty Fortress Is Our God":

> The heauens and the fyrmamente,
>   do wonderfully declare:
> The glory of God omnipotent,
>   hys woorkes and what they are.
> Eche day declareth by hys course,
>   an other day to come:
> And by the nyght we know lykewise,
>   a nyghtly course to runne. (STC 2420)

Although Sidney's first two stanzas are also absolutely regular, they contain differentiating touches which are typical of his ver-

sions: the use of feminine endings; the use of "like-sounding
wordes"—especially in the internal rhymes of the first and third
lines—; and a more careful attention to content than to steady
beat. In fact, in the years around 1579, Sidney believed that the
essence of vernacular poetry resided in sounds and syllable count,
not in accent:

> 1 The heavnly Frame sets forth the Fame
>   Of him that only thunders;
>   The firmament, so strangely bent,
>   Shewes his handworking wonders.
> 2 Day unto day doth it display,
>   Their Course doth it acknowledg,
>   And night to night succeeding right
>   In darkness teach cleere knowledg.

The placing of "only" in line two for regularity tends to make the
statement imply just the opposite of what is really meant; each
"it" in lines five and six awkwardly refers to "wonders"; the metaphysical gesture in line eight is simply ambiguous; and feminine
endings are more often a weakening, not a strengthening, factor
in English poetry.

Unstressed endings are necessary, however, in truly trochaic
verse, but even this stanza from Psalm 42 is not wholly trochaic:

> As the chafed hart which brayeth
> Seeking some refreshing brook,
> So my soul in panting playeth,
> Thirsting on my God to look.
>   My soul thirsts indeed in me
>   After ever living thee;
>   Ah, when comes my blessed being,
>   Of Thy face to have a seing?

The important thing to remember is not that this final couplet is
terrible, but that Sidney relentlessly forced himself to try pattern
after pattern through forty-three poems before he tired. None of
them really has life:

> The lord the lord my shepheard is,
>   And so can never I
>   Tast misery.

And the reason for the lack of vitality is easy to find: the maintenance of regularity and rhyme is everywhere more important than meaning. Thus filler words, perverted syntax, and rhyme without reason are characteristic of Sidney's Psalms. But the effort surely was not without reward, for Sidney discovered that the life of poetry did not lie in lengths of line, or in symmetry, to use Robert Montgomery's apt term. Perhaps Sidney sought the answer next in the principle of length of syllable, or quantity.

III   Quantitative Verse

The so-called "first" generation of Humanists—such as Linacre, Grocyn, Colet, and More—were primarily interested in learning Greek, in purifying Latin, and in recovering and restoring texts; but the "second" generation—such as Elyot, Cheke, Ascham, and Watson—in addition to their continuing interest in textual scholarship, were primarily interested in programs and procedures which would allow the discoveries of the new learning to enrich and improve education. Essentially, this meant the use of Classical authors in English classrooms as texts for grammar, rhetoric, and logic, both for "matter" and "manner." Just as the doctrine of imitation led to a great amount of translation back and forth between Latin and English—the translations of Virgil being typical school exercises—so also were the attempts to write quantitative English poetry. In this vein, Ascham could praise Chaucer, Wyatt, Surrey, Norton, and Phaer for undertaking translation, but chastise them for not trying quantity: "but, if soch good wittes and forward diligence had bene directed to follow the best examples, and not have bene caryed by tyme and custome, to content themselves with that barbarous and rude Ryming, emonges their other worthy praises, which they have justly deserved, this had not bene the least, to be counted emonges men of learning and skill, more like unto the Grecians, than unto the Gothians, in the handling of their verse."[5]

Elizabethans generally learned that trying to domesticate quantity was a hopeless pursuit when Richard Stanyhurst published his first four books of the *Aeneid* in 1582, prefaced by a full explanation of the rules of "art" by which his translation was made. Although he made himself a laughing stock, Thomas Campion at the end of the century was still calling loudly for a return to quantity, a call answered by Samuel Daniel, who took delight in pointing out the ironic fact that Campion was himself one of England's most accomplished composers of accentual syllabic verse.

Samuel Daniel (who first found favor from the Countess of Pembroke) deserves a settled place in the history of English criticism because he grounded his *Defence of Ryme* (1603) in the very custom and nature which Ascham would suppress—"Custome that is before all Law, Nature that is above all Arte." Daniel addressed himself to the Countess's son, William Herbert: "The Generall Custome, and use of Ryme in this kingdome, Noble Lord, having beene so long (as if from a Graunt of Nature) held unquestionable, made me to imagine that it lay altogither out of the way of contradiction, and was become so natural, as we should never have had a thought to cast it off into reproch, or be made to thinke that it ill-became our language." Here Daniel speaks within the great developing tradition of Sidney, Dryden, Johnson, Wordsworth, Arnold, and Eliot; but in specifics he is well ahead of Sidney, for he realized that rime *per se,* rather than being what Sidney called the "chiefe life" of English poetry, could be dispensed with. Still, English poetry "most religiously respects the accent."[6] (But then Daniel had listened to Shakespeare.)

Even though the attempt to compose quantitatively was in the end useless because the dominant aspect of English is accent (or stress, or pitch), the fact that we still talk in our schoolrooms of "long" and "short" syllables shows how intense and pervasive was the attempt to write English along Latin lines. Lacking full awareness of the nature of their new language, however, academics advocated, and poets attempted, quantity; and this attempt led them to a discovery about a previously unacknowledged aspect of their language—rhythm.

The attempt among serious poets to impose quantity on English was short-lived, but well publicized, thanks to Harvey and Spenser, and well documented, positively and negatively. After Spenser had told Harvey in the October, 1579, letter about Sidney's and Dyer's banning all "bald Rymers," he went on to say that they have "prescribed certaine Lawes and rules of Quantities of English sillables for English Verse: having had thereof already greate practise," and that he himself is, "of late, more in love with my Englishe Versifying than with Ryming." His guide, he says in an earlier letter, was Sidney, who gave him a set of rules which he had received from Thomas Drant, a London preacher, and which Sidney had in turn modified. (Drant's own extant poetry, ironically, is in fourteeners.)

Of Sidney's thirteen quantitative poems (out of 281 canonical poems), only one was written before the *Old Arcadia* (1578–80) and one after: his experiments were few and soon over. After his first attempt (OA 11), an elegiac sung by the prince Musidorus in the "First Eclogues," there is appended in an early manuscript of the *Old Arcadia* some "Nota" which Ringler believes are these rules of Sidney, mentioned by Spenser. Ringler, who has analyzed Sidney's quantitative poetry more extensively and favorably than anyone else, believes that all of Sidney's quantitative verse except CS 5, which he dates 1578 or earlier, can be scanned according to these rules. Still, Ringler admits that "when read aloud many of his lines do not sound like verse to English ears" (392). And as an example I cite an elegiac, CS 13:

Unto no body my woman saith she had rather a wife be,
   Then to my selfe, not though *Jove* grew a suter of hers.
These be her words, but a woman's words to a love that is eager,
   In wind or water streame do require to be writ.

But the saving factor is that all of the quantitative poems and almost all of the accentual-syllabic ones in the *Old Arcadia* are intended as songs; therefore the structure of the setting, whether real or imagined, reinforces the meter, or compensates for the lack of it, in the poems.

The close alliance between music and poetry was taken for granted during the sixteenth century. Indeed, a distinguishing characteristic of that century was the development of the native lyric tradition from Wyatt in the court of Henry VIII through Campion and the other great Elizabethan poet-composers. What is remarkable about Sidney, then, is his eventual development of a poetic theory entirely divorced from music. When Lalus and Dicus debate the relative merits of quantitative and accentual-syllabic poetry in the *Old Arcadia,* each agrees that setting is important; but Dicus, the Classicist, says that the music is the more important while Lalus, the defender of rime, believes the opposite. That this debate, occurring at the end of the "First Eclogues," is suppressed in all manuscripts which can be dated after 1580 is important because, taken along with the fact that Sidney's rules, or "Nota," appear only in a manuscript which has to be dated between 1580 and 1582, this double suppression indicates that Sidney quickly lost interest in the attempt to adopt Latin measures.

The suppression surely shows, too, as Ringler suggests, that the points raised were incorporated in *The Defence of Poesie* (1580–81). But what is remarkable about the discussion of the relative merits of "verse" and "rime" in the *Defence* is that there is no mention made of music in connection with rime because Sidney was discovering that poetry could incorporate its own music through rhythm. Part of his discovery of the rhythms of language surely must have come, as Theodore Spencer and John Thompson have cogently argued, from Sidney's experiments with Classical meter, though these were few in number. That Sidney took the experiments seriously can be told in part from the awe expressed by, and similar attempts of, Spenser. More significant is the fact that only the nobles and Philisides are permitted to sing quantitative verse in the *Old Arcadia*. Yet more significant in the other direction is that the only quantitative line written by Sidney after 1579–80 is a hexameter for the foolish Dametas in the *New Arcadia* (OP 2):

Miso mine owne pigsnie thou shalt heare news o' *Damaetas.*

This does not merely ridicule Dametas's typical pretentiousness, but is as well a delightful confession that quantity could not produce English poetry.

IV   *Imitations, Foreign and Native*

More important in the development of Sidney's poetic than these Latin imitations were his imitations of Italian poetry, works which have been analysed and discussed thoroughly and well by Robert Montgomery and David Kalstone. Kalstone limits himself to the poems of the *Old Arcadia* (unfortunately, treating them in the contexts of the *Arcadia* of 1593 which was put together by the Countess of Pembroke), and he ignores the important collection of poems called *Certaine Sonets,* a collection which parallels on a small scale the poetry of the *Old Arcadia*: both contain native iambic songs, sonnets, quantitative verse, and translations or adaptations of Latin and Continental poetry.

Although the variety of poems in the *Old Arcadia* is impressively great, they all are to an extent the prisoners of context. No matter how good they are, they still subsume a greater purpose, either that of the narrative or that of the pastoral eclogues. In general, they fall into two kinds: lyric and formal. Among the first are such fine pieces as "My true love hath my heart," and among the latter the much-praised double-sestina "Yee Gote-heard Gods." The first or lyric kind can be very good, but none is extraordinary; whereas the second or formal kind can be extraordinary, but not good *as poetry*—as *tours de force,* yes, but not as poetry. Even William Empson, among the first to single out "Yee Gote-heard Gods" for praise, has to admit that the poem is "foreign to the normal modes or later developments of the language," and that "it beats, however rich its orchestration, with a wailing and immovable monotony, for ever upon the same doors in vain."[7] Kalstone's praise is the most favorable of any of the critics, but his concentration is on content and modulations of mood, not on poetics. Of such a poem, we can most fruitfully agree with Robert Montgomery in his summation of Sidney's early poetry: "stylistically the poem still remains symmetrical, amplified, ornate, which should warn us that these qualities do not always force simplicity or intensity of statement alone. These results are merely the normal limits of amplified discourse as Sidney practices it in the *Arcadia* poems, and 'You Gote-heard Gods' is a fine demonstration that limits exist to be transgressed" (47).

That all of the *Certaine Sonets* were written during the years of the *Old Arcadia,* but not included in it, indicates that in writing them Sidney was not concerned with problems of discourse. As can be expected (and as is true of those of the *Old Arcadia*), the poems deal generally and broadly with love; but they tell no "story." To be sure, when Sidney first got them ready for scribal transcription, he put at the end two sonnets which reject secular love, "Thou blind man's marke" and "Leave me ô love"; later, for another transcription, he added two at the beginning which invoke love. Thus there is a contour of sorts to the group, but what makes the poems interesting and important in the study of Sidney is their actual lack of context, thus allowing us to get closer to Sidney the poet than we can in any other poems, and what we discover are the first signs of a developing "voice."

By "voice" I simply mean that distinctive quality which completes a poem, which makes it hang together, which makes it sing. Sidney uses two terms which are pertinent: in the *Defence* he calls this quality *"energia"* and in Sonnet 15 of *Astrophel and Stella* he calls it "inward tuch." One either has the quality innately or he does not, but to have it innately does not make one a poet, as Dylan Thomas did not live to learn. Rather, poetry comes with discipline, with the mastery of the craft. As Sidney says in the *Defence*:

> *Poesie* must not be drawne by the eares, it must be gently led, or rather it must lead, which was partly the cause that made the auncient learned affirme, it was a divine gift & no humane skil; since all other knowledges lie readie for anie that have strength of wit: A *Poet* no industrie can make, if his owne *Genius* be not carried into it. And therefore is an old Proverbe, *Orator fit, Poeta nascitur.* Yet confesse I alwaies, that as the fertilest ground must be manured, so must the highest flying wit have a *Dedalus* to guide him. That *Dedalus,* they say both in this and in other, hath three wrings to beare it selfe up into the ayre of due commendation: that is Art, Imitation, and Exercise. (III, 37)

Sidney's own development is proof of the validity of the requirements: his education gave him the tools, his work with the Psalms, with quantity, with foreign (in the full sense) forms, and the demands of the various contexts of the *Old Arcadia* made him a poet. The full development of Sidney's "voice" is revealed in *Astrophel and Stella,* but it begins to stir in the *Certaine Sonets.*

Poem 18, a sonnet, is a good one to look at, for it may be said to be transitional: it is essentially formal—correlative verse—but is so completely controlled that the art is almost entirely hidden, the thirteenth line coming not just as a surprise but in itself is so under the hand of the poet that it leads into the fourteenth line, which is the climax and summation of the poem:

> In wonted walkes, since wonted fancies change,
> >   Some cause there is, which of strange cause doth rise:
> For in each thing wherto mine eye doth range,
> >   Part of my paine me seemes engraved lyes.
> The Rockes which were of constant mind the marke
> >   In clyming steepe, now hard refusall show:
> The shading woods seeme now my Sunne to darke,
> >   And stately hilles disdaine to looke so low.
> The restfull Caves now restlesse visions give,
> >   In Dales I see each way a hard assent:

Like late mowne meades, late cut from joy I live.
Alas sweete Brookes do in my tears augment:
Rockes, woods, hilles, caves, dales, meads, brookes, answere me,
  infected mindes infect each thing they see.

What is new in this poem is a single voice of meditation which sustains the movement to the climax. The voice is hesitating, to be sure: "which of strange cause doth rise," "The shading woods seeme now my Sunne to darke," and other phrases reveal bare meter standing out. But, for the most part, playing over the regular beat of the meter is rhythm—the sound of an actual voice working its way through thought. Only a poet fully in control would dare "Rockes, woods, hilles, caves, dales, meads, brookes, answere me," and then follow it with the absolutely suspended "Infected mindes infect each thing they see." Each line is essentially iambic pentameter, but the voice of the poem is so established that the reverberations between meter and rhythm are so felt that poetry is realized.

The essential discovery was that substitutions necessary to meaning do not destroy the metrical base, but enhance it by the simultaneous creation of rhythm: "Part of" in line four, for example, is trochaic. Furthermore, the voice can rise in pitch over absolute meter: "For in each thing" and "Like late mowne meades" are phrases made up of two iambic, accentual-syllabic feet; but the rhythm in each case increases in pitch over each syllable.

The most complete poem which Sidney wrote before *Astrophel and Stella* is "Thou blind man's marke" (CS 31):

Thou blind man's marke, thou foole's selfe chosen snare,
Fond fancie's scum, and dregs of scattred thought,
Band of all evils, cradle of causelesse care,
Thou web of will, whose end is never wrought;
Desire, desire I have too dearely bought,
With price of mangled mind thy worthlesse ware,
Too long, too long asleepe thou hast me brought,
Who should my mind to higher things prepare.
But yet in vaine thou hast my ruine sought,
In vaine thou madest me to vaine things aspire,
In vaine thou kindlest all thy smokie fire;

> For vertue hath this better lesson taught,
> Within my selfe to seeke my onelie hire:
> Desiring nought but how to kill desire.

The tone of the speaker's voice moves from sarcastic disgust in the first quatrain describing "desire," through a sense of superiority and triumph in the second, a sense which is almost frantically so in the first three lines of the sestet, but which comes under full control with lines twelve and thirteen. To this point, the poem is a good poem; and, in thought, it is a completed poem, but only a conventional one, much as is the whole poem, its companion piece, "Leave me ô love" (CS 32). A poem can be conventional and still be good, even great. Here, in fact, the voice so far has been so strong and vivid that we do not realize in reading that the only departures from the iambic pentametric norm are the two trochees in line three, which intensify the bitterness and anger of the first quatrain. By lines twelve and thirteen, the bitterness and anger seem to have been repressed and replaced by philosophic calm and rational control. But what makes the poem great is the last, quiet, ironic line which, after the poem is over, forces us to contemplate the complexity of that paradox, man the rational animal.

In a chapter as fragmented as this has been and as short as it must be, full attention cannot be paid to the variety of Sidney's poetry from 1578 to 1580. Furthermore, we must keep in mind that—in addition to the poems of the *Old Arcadia,* the "Eclogues," the Psalms, the *Certaine Sonets,* and possibly some few other poems—Sidney was immersed in the prose-narrative of the *Old Arcadia* and was formulating his answer to Gosson, whether in mind or on paper. In what may have been not much more than some thirty months, Sidney moved from the facile and jejune *The Lady of May* to a point where he was prepared to start *Astrophel and Stella,* one of the great works of English literature. During that short time he accomplished as much in volume, diversity, and quality as would have, and has, satisfied many a writer during a whole lifetime.

This catalytic moment in Sidney's literary career was also Spenser's. He, too, during this time had written an essay on poetry; he, too, had before and again during this period, worked with Continental forms; he, too, tried his hand at quantity; and his *Shepheardes Calender* was a conscious attempt to work within tradition, both esoteric and natural, Chaucerian and native, exploring old themes in an established genre, and searching for the music of the English line in essentially rhythmic meter. As poetry, none of this work came to much: *The Shepheardes Calender* is extraordinary but, if I be not deceived, hath but little poetry in it. Like "Yee Gote-heard Gods," one appreciates it cerebrally, not viscerally. But all of the efforts were ultimately fruitful. These were, after all, the years as well during which Spenser was already at work on *The Fairie Queene*. We hesitate to consider what the course of English literature would have been had all the talk and productivity of 1579 somehow not taken place.

CHAPTER 5

Astropel and Stella

*A*strophel and Stella is one of the world's great collections of lyric poetry. As a categorical consequence, it is as well one of the world's great sonnet sequences. But, when this second fact is acknowledged, the first is obscured unless we understand that a sonnet sequence *is* essentially a collection of lyric poetry, a collection special in form because of its biographical, or narrative, guise. To assume the reverse, that a sequence is essentially biography, or narrative, merely in poetic form may have its appeals and rewards; but it does the poet a disservice.

Surely all poets write from experience, but experience can be active and passive, immediate and detached, imagined and actual, felt and contemplated—and aspects of all of these in various quantities and combinations. As a result, to say that a poet had to have a specific kind of love experience to write a certain kind of love poetry makes as much sense as saying that Shakespeare must have committed murder because he wrote poetry of blood guilt. As Robert Henryson so delightfully put the case, "Quha wait gif all that Chauceir wrait was trew?" (*The Testament of Cresseid*).

Still, believing that all that Sidney wrote in *Astrophel and Stella* was true is paying him high compliment. It means that he achieved the poetic sincerity, or wholeness, or completeness, for which poets strive. To be more specific, it means that in this sequence Sidney created poem after poem in which the voice, as I have defined the term, is so realized that we take it for his. In short, Sidney showed his fellows how to combine meter and rhythm in creating poetry that moves, instructs, and delights.

I *Meter and Rhythm*

When measured against the poetry of his predecessors, except for Wyatt, and even against his own early poetry, the rhythmical achievement of Sidney in this sonnet sequence is overwhelming.

As a case in point, and as a key to unlocking the sequence, let us analyze the meter and rhythm of sonnet 47. The scansion of the poem goes:[1]

> What, have/I thus/betrayed/my lib/ertie?
> Can those/blacke beames/such burn/ing markes/engrave
> In my/free side?/or am/I borne/a slave,
> Whose necke/becomes/such yoke/of tyr/anny?
> Or want/I sense/to feele/my mis/erie?
> Or sprite,/disdaine/of such/disdaine/to have?
> *Who for*/long faith,/tho day/ly helpe/I crave,
> May get/no almes/but scorne/of beg/gerie.
> *Vertue*/awake,/*Beautie*/but beau/tie is.
> I may,/I must,/I can,/I will,/I do
> Leave fol/*lowing that,*/which it/is gaine/to misse.
> *Let her*/go. Soft,/but here/she comes./Go to,
> Unkind,/I love/you not:/O me,/that eye
> Doth make/my heart/*give to*/my tongue/the lie.

Each unitalicized foot is perfectly iambic, having two syllables, the second of which receives (*within that foot*) relatively more stress than the first syllable. This basic meter is interrupted five times by reversed, or trochaic, feet, and once by a tripping anapest in line eleven, the first syllable of which is barely audible, if at all, for the word "following" is usually slurred, "fol'wing."

This last statement encroaches on the realm of rhythm, and shows that meter and rhythm are abstract terms about poetic qualities which are inseparable; for rhythm is the actual movement of metrical feet in coordination with one another. These feet are, after all, more than mere pairs (and triads) of relatively stressed syllables: each can be parts of a longer word ("ertie"), one word ("betrayed"), one word and a part of another ("my lib"), or two words ("what, have") (all from line one). Furthermore, some feet (as feet), take longer to say; some receive relatively little overall stress in a line; and most are not syntactically complete (an exception is a foot such as "Go to"). Thus rhythm is the actual speaking or meditating voice moving through the poem over, against, and through the meter. This fact, as Robert Frost said in *The Figure A Poem Makes,* is the essential one of lyric poetry: "The possibilities for tune from the dramatic tones of meaning struck across the rigidity of a limited meter are endless."

Whereas meter can be graphically indicated, rhythm cannot. To mark rhythm, we should have signs to indicate pitch, stress, juncture, duration, and such basic tones as interrogatory, exclamatory, assertive, and imperative. But no one system of description has ever been established. The need is great, and perhaps the structural linguists will turn their attention to this positive question and away from the negative one of denying the fact of the metrical base of traditional English poetry from Sidney, through Pope and Wordsworth, to Robert Frost and many contemporary writers. There are, have been, and will be other meters, but the fact remains that most English poetry from the Renaissance to the present is accentual-syllabic. But the fact will remain obscured and debated until we learn (through the eye) to hear both the meter and the rhythm simultaneously. In a schoolboy's rendition of a memorized poem, we hear meter; in an Actor's Studio presentation of Shakespeare's blank verse, we hear rhythms; but, in Sir John Gielgud's, we hear both.

Without cluttering the page with an elaborate system of notation, perhaps the following breaking of the lines of Sonnet 47 and the use of only two marks of stress will at least be helpful in indicating rhythm:

What,?
          x
     have I thus
           betrayed my líberty?

Can those bláck beámes (?)
     such burning markes engrave
            In my free side?

or am Í born a sláve, (?) x
    whose nécke becomes such yóke of tyranny?

       x
Or want Í sense (to feele my miserie)? Or sprite?
(Distaine of such distaine to have)

       x
Whó for long faith
   (tho dayly helpe I crave)

       x
May gét nó almes
       x
    but scórne of béggerie.

     x
Vértue awake!

Béautie but beautie ís!

> I may
>   I must
>   I can
>   I will
>   I dó
>   x   x
> Leave, following that,
>   which it is gáine to mísse.
>
>   ́   x
> Let her go!
>
> Sóft,
>
> but here she comes.
>
>   x
> "Go to,   ́
>   Unkind!
> I love you not."
> O
>   mé ́
>   x   x
>   that eye Doth make my heart
>   x   x
> give to my tongue
>
>   x
>   the lie.

Perfectly heard is the self-questioning, self-assertive, self-mocking voice of Astrophel, Sidney's wholly realized Petrarchan, a poet-lover-Platonist.

II *Petrarchism*

Petrarchism is a lyric, abstract, attitude toward love which rightly takes its name from the fourteenth-century poet who brought together and unified a rich variety of poetic-love attitudes in his *Rime*. While Petrarch was simply a man who wrote poetry, the end result was a synthesis and amalgamation of traditions to which succeeding poets could turn; and one man's invention thus became convention for others.

Conventional poetry is not necessarily bad poetry, but it tends to be quite ordinary if the poet simply follows lines drawn by others. To reiterate, the challenge to the Elizabethan poet was not to do something never done before, but to show how well in his own imitation, through art and exercise, he could take what *had* been done before and make it his own. But, when it came to writing Petrarchan sonnets, the challenge was great indeed. On the one hand, the body of thought known as "Petrarchism" is highly stylized and in the end negative; on the other, the sonnet is a highly disciplined, sophisticated form. Thus, when routinely executed, a Petrarchan sonnet can be merely pretentious; when well done, it can be truly metaphysical because of the rich philosophical heritage of the content and the demands of the form.

Isolating the elements of Petrarchism is as difficult as marking off a spectrum, so well do the constituents merge. Its emphasis on the external and internal glory of the beloved is as old as the Song of Songs, the catalogues of which received new definition in the romance poetry of Provençe, which added the idea of service to that of adoration. This addition led, in turn, to the more formalized poetry of the Court of Love with its inevitable comparisons of the moods of the lover to aspects of nature and to meditations on mutability and eternity. As a result, erotic though it was in fact, the poetry of the Court of Love was Christianized, as was, but not so easily, the Song of Songs.

Because of the obvious erotic nature of the Song of Songs, the theologians of the Middle Ages pressed hard to find an allegorical meaning in order to justify its canonical existence. Its blatant sexuality is more in keeping with the outright "pagan" love poetry of Classical Rome which celebrated such loves as that of Mars and Venus. But this kind of poetry also rapidly developed into a convention, the Cult of Cupid, and was made safe; for Cupid seemed to have more leaden-headed arrows in his quiver than golden, and the cult was more concerned with the frustrations of love—the anguish, the sleeplessness, and the melancholy—than with its success.

Along with the biblical, romance, and Classical elements, another part of Petrarchism, Neo-Platonism, justifies the service and worship aspects of the Court of Love, and rationalizes the fatal and unfruitful aspects of the Cult of Cupid. Basic to Neo-Platonism is the separation of the flesh and the spirit, the first being bad and earthy; the second, good and heavenly. Attendant to this dichotomy is the feeling that love is essentially spiritual; an interanimation, it is consummated not by the meeting of bodies but by that of souls and minds. As a result of this heritage, Petrarchism is filled on one hand with the variety of debates between reason and will, heart and soul, eye and mind, and, on the other hand, with the belief that love somehow can transcend the body and lead by stages to a completely ecstatic, rapturous, other-world experience. And here, as in the Court of Love, the inferences necessary for a Christian interpretation are slight and obvious.

Petrarchism so partakes of all this heritage, however, that who is to say what causes a lover's crying out for sleep to come: Cupid's leaden dart, the unobtainable lady who still must be served, or guilty pricks of conscience?

The first signs of the shaping of this varied heritage into a poetic form of fourteen lines can be seen in the early thirteenth century in Sicily, and the development is quickly found in Italy, so that by the end of the century Dante is at work on his *Vita nuova,* which is predominantly prose and contains only twenty-five "true" sonnets of love, has six other love poems, and twenty-five on various subjects and in various kinds of form. Yet in the work of Dante the variety of traditions comes together in a focus on the concept of the beloved's being herself a reflection of Transcendent Beauty, so that her love returned could ultimately confirm a blessing such as that which Beatrice's leads to in *La Commedia.*

But the idea that earthy love can lead to purification receives its fullest lyric definition in the fourteenth century within Petrarch's two sequences of three hundred and seventeen sonnets in the *Rime,* which added the final touch and distinguishing characteristic to Petrarchism: the celebrating of love through a series of fourteen-line poems which have a kind of unity because most, *but not all,* are written to or about one woman. The relationship between Petrarch and Laura may have been protracted (they met in 1327, and she died in 1348), but it was never intimate for two reasons, as Morris Bishop has so cogently argued: the two were of different social positions, and she was married all, and pregnant and nursing most, of the time. Bishop's summary of their relationship in *Petrarch and His World* (1963) is worth repeating because it indicates, even in the archetypal sequence, the place and real value of the "lady": "He loved her in the poet's way, as woman, as goddess, as Muse. Laura, esteeming her own little personality as something of value, resented his using her for copy; she did not realize that he loved her in part because he could use her for copy. . . . For him the proof of his love was her stimulation of his spirit to the production of poetic fruit; and indeed that seems excellent proof" (158).

Where Sidney learned his Petrarchism is unimportant because the sources were numerous and, circularly, *Astrophel and Stella* is proof that he did. The poetic results of Wyatt's visit to Italy and the imitations by Surrey were available in Tottel. While Sidney was in Italy, the bookstalls were filled with volumes of sonnets. The Pléiade in France was simultaneously totally involved with Petrarch, and in 1569 Spenser had translated some Petrarch *and* Du Bellay. And, at the same time Sidney was writing sonnets, so was his acquaintance Thomas Watson, whose *Hecatompathia, or Passionate Century of Love* was published in 1582, thus becoming the "first" sequence in England. The poems, eighteen lines long, are openly indebted to Continental sources and are unevenly experimental. Thus, Watson's is "a first" in one sense only, for Sidney's is the first English sequence which frankly undertook to imitate the Petrarchan convention; and his success is proved by the fact that, when it was published in 1591, after circulating in manuscript form, *Astrophel and Stella* triggered an explosion of sonneteering which in bulk and quality may be appalling from our point of view, but which in significance cannot be overestimated: Sidney taught a whole generation how to write English poetry. (Interestingly, Watson's posthumously published sequence of 1594 contains only fourteen-line poems.)

Astrophel and Stella is, then, highly conventional poetry.[2] Stella —the beautiful, attracting, yet distant beloved—and Astrophel— the clever, witty, long-suffering, courtly, imaginative, intelligent, passionate, yet ultimately rejected lover—are both pure stereotype; the subjects, themes, and range of the sequence are all derivative; but everything comes alive in Sidney's art.

III   *Poet and Speaker*

In light of the analysis of Sidney's ability to create voice and from the examination of the heritage of the sequence, we are in a position to see the justice of David Kalstone's remark that: "In Astrophel, the complex, questioning hero in love, Sidney found an excellent persona; for Astrophel has no one stance, but moves flexibly among a number of changing attitudes. Only momentarily can he entertain the Petrarchan vision of earthly beauty that restores the lover to grace or wisdom. His significant activity is the discovery of conflict, and he delights in it" (180).

But it is only Astrophel the persona who sees no resolution to the conflict of love. In the end, even Kalstone mistakes Astrophel's ideas for Sidney's. We may grant that the name "Astrophel" means "star-lover," as does Philisides; but the name "Astrophel" cannot be deduced from "Philip Sidney." The voice is "real," but it is not really Sidney's, though, of course, the ultimate control is entirely his.

Not to be alert for this duality is to be in danger of missing complexity. In Sonnet 10, for example, the surface movement of the poem is that of a simple diatribe by Astrophel against Reason, one which ends with Reason's subjugation. But the actual movement is such that the final joke is on Astrophel, not Reason:

> Reason, in faith thou art well serv'd, that still
> Wouldst brabling be with sence and love in me:
> I rather wisht thee clime the Muses's hill,
> Or reach the fruite of Nature's choisest tree,
>   Or seeke heavn's course, or heavn's inside to see:
> Why shouldst thou toyle our thornie soile to till?
> Leave sense, and those which sense's objects be:
> Deale thou with powers of thoughts, leave love to will.
>   But thou wouldst needs fight both with love and sence,
> With sword of wit, giving wounds of dispraise,
> Till downe-right blowes did foyle thy cunning fence:
> For soone as they strake thee with *Stella's* rayes,
>   Reason thou kneel'dst, and offeredst straight to prove
>   By reason good, good reason her to love.

To Astrophel reason is merely a quality of mind; hence, its constructs, especially Neo-Platonism, prove inadequate in life when the facts and products of other human attributes cannot be accommodated within them. But to Sidney, as to Hooker, reason had a much greater meaning. To them, reason was the essential basis of human life, that which *joins* man's multiple qualities, qualities which Astrophel's kind of reason would *divide* under headings like "body" and "soul." Thus, Sidney can show Astrophel's Byronic delight in discovery of life's delusions and, at the same time, show him as blind to the principles of natural law.

The evidence is not simply relegated to the last line, where Sidney emphasizes by word choice and inverted repetition the concept of right reason within which a first principle is that consummated, fruitful love is good, the highest human good. Rather, in a second reading of the poem, we tend to experience a pun even in the first line, where "in faith" may be more than Astrophel's casual expletive and be the first indication of the poet's larger, theological orientation. Such an interpretation is certainly made clear, however, by line six: "Why shouldst thou toyle our thornie soile to till?" The line is purposely, perceptibly slowed in order to force attention to the answer implied: why? because God cursed the ground at Adam's fall so that it would bring forth thorns and thistles, forcing Adam to till it and to sweat daily for his bread. And Astrophel's error is manifested in the next two lines: because choice is a rational obligation not a willful relinquishment, reason must face squarely the facts of the flesh. Indeed, the collective end of poetry, philosophy, astronomy, and theology (the burden of lines three, four, and five) is not cultivation of the mind, but of the whole man. And precisely for this total commitment, Reason "wouldest needs fight," where in line nine Sidney makes a double point—revealing both Astrophel's scorn and the underlying principle of moral necessity—through a masterful use of a rising pitch in the rhythm over the first two feet. After this line Sidney seemingly gives Astrophel his head, allowing him to play upon lesser aspects of reason, but through words which have their roots in *witan* and *cunnan,* two Anglo-Saxon words meaning "to know." Through this device, then, far from giving Astrophel the advantage in these lines, Sidney prepares for the last two lines wherein the concepts of knowledge and generation merge movingly within an ancient tradition.

IV *The Sequence*

Because of a controlling overview of his own, Sidney is able, then, to allow Astrophel to stand forth as the perfect Petrarchan: poet-lover-Platonist. By now it should be clear that such a statement is not denigrating. In fact, Astrophel comes close to being Sidney in all three of his roles as poet, as lover, as philosopher.

One tenth of the sequence is poems on poetry, starting with the justly famous first one, a *tour de force* which advocates a plain, direct, unadorned style, in carefully contrived, balanced, highly rhetorical lines of hexameter. But in this poem "Invention" is called "Nature's child," and its source is placed in the poet, not in "others' leaves." In AS 3 derivative imitation is left to others:

> For me in sooth, no Muse but one I know:
> Phrases and Problemes from my reach do grow,

And strange things cost too deare for my poore spirites.
How then? even thus: in *Stella's* face I reed,
What Love and Beautie be, then all my deed
But Copying is, what in her Nature writes.

But this poem does more than advocate directness; it sets up Stella
as the image of love and beauty within a Platonic frame of reference. Thus the poem goes beyond Sidney's to Astrophel's poetic.
These two aspects of Astrophel's poetic come together again in
AS 15:

You that do search for everie purling spring,
Which from the ribs of old *Parnassus* flowes,
And everie floure, not sweet perhaps, which growes
Neare therabout, into your Poesie wring;
You that do Dictionarie's methode bring
Into your rimes, running in ratling rowes:
You that poore *Petrarch's* long deceased woes,
With new-borne sighes and denisend wit do sing;
You take wrong waies, those far-fet helpes be such,
As do bewray a want of inward tuch:
And sure at length stolne goods do come to light.
But if (both for your love and skill) your name
You seeke to nurse at fullest breasts of Fame,
Stella behold, and then begin to endite.

The speaker is Sidney to the extent that the ideas reinforce those
already seen in the *Defence,* but they are not Sidney's to the extent
that he knew full well, as would indeed any reader of his day,
that the sequence was fully based on "poore *Petrarch's* long deceased woes." Yet, he also knew that the success of the sequence
resided in execution, in setting up an Astrophel who was unique.
Astrophel had, at the same time, to be worth attending so that the
control and voice in many poems is such that we do not trouble
to distinguish between poet and persona; the poem simply is good,
as in the case of AS 44—

My words I know do well set forth my mind,
My mind bemones his sense of inward smart;
Such smart may pitie claime of any hart,
Her heart, sweete heart, is of no Tygre's kind:
Any yet she heares, yet I no pitty find;

> But more I crie, lesse grace she doth impart,
>   Alas, what cause is there so overthwart,
> That Noblenesse it selfe makes thus unkind?
>   I much do guesse, yet find no truth save this,
> That when the breath of my complaints doth tuch
> Those daintie dores unto the Court of blisse,
>   The heav'nly nature of that place is such,
>   That once come there, the sobs of mine annoyes
>   Are metamorphosd straight to tunes of joyes.

Many of the famous poems of the sequence may, and should, be read in this neutral manner; for example, "With how sad steps, ô moon, thou climb'st the skies" (AS 31), "Come sleep, ô sleep, the certaine knot of peace" (AS 39), "Having this day my horse, my hand, my launce" (AS 41), "In Martiall sports I had my cunning tride" (AS 53), and "Thought with good cause thou likest so well the night" (AS 96). Such poems are partly conventional, but they are more because they bear Sidney's special mark. They are urbane, even, and under full control in a cavalier, courtly way.

Some poems filled with convention such as AS 17, even though they are spoken by Astrophel, show no sign of duality between poet and speaker:

> His mother deare *Cupid* offended late,
>   Because that *Mars,* growne slacker in her love,
>   With pricking shot he did not throughly move,
> To keepe the pace of their first loving state.
> The boy refusde for feare of *Marse's* hate,
>   Who threatened stripes, if he his wrath did prove:
>   But she in chafe him from her lap did shove,
> Brake bow, brake shafts, while *Cupid* weeping sate:
>   Till that his grandame *Nature* pittying it,
> Of *Stella's* browes made him two better bowes,
> And in her eyes of arrowes infinit.
>   O how for joy he leapes, ô how he crowes,
>   And straight therewith, like wags new got to play,
>   Fals to shrewd turnes, and I was in his way.

While nothing is directly stated, the implied comment on love is deep, and the poem delights.

In a poem like AS 17, Astrophel wittily laughs at himself; in other poems, he becomes a wise observer, both of the human scene and of himself, as is caught in AS 5:

> It is most true, that eyes are form'd to serve
> The inward light: and that the heavenly part
> Ought to be king, from whose rules who do swerve,
> Rebels to Nature, strive for their owne smart.
>   It is most true, what we call *Cupid's* dart,
> An image is, which for our selves we carve;
> And, fooles, adore in temple of our hart,
> Till that good God make Church and Churchman starve.
>   True, that true Beautie Vertue is indeed,
> Whereof this Beautie can be but a shade,
> Which elements with mortall mixture breed:
> True, that on earth we are but pilgrims made,
>   And should in soule up to our countrey move:
> True, and yet true that I must *Stella* love.

Even when these truths are fully recognized and Astrophel concludes, "and yet true that I must *Stella* love," there is little separation between the poet and the speaker; but there is some. Astrophel feelingly seems to understand that to acknowledge distinctions between truths does not necessarily rid one of one of them, while Sidney may know that distinctions can be in contradiction without leading to mutual exclusion. Our life is not so.

As a love poem, Sonnet 5 has interesting implications. As a poem by Sidney the context suggests that Stella is not a worthy love, that to love her is against Nature, that the love is pagan, and that her beauty somehow does not partake of the heavenly. Yet, in context Stella is of a set value that is good and positive; she is the true Book of Nature, created by a Heavenly Author. Thus, we sense Sidney the creator lapse for a moment; and, if by any chance a *real* Stella was the point of departure for the *ideal* one, her portrait in the sequence is far from life.

As a love poem by Astrophel, however, the poem must be read differently; for we must take Stella as a standard of excellence, as a dark lady in appearance only. So understood, Astrophel is seen caught in a typical Petrarchan pose; he feels somehow that love is irrational, fanciful, of the will and flesh, and, therefore, bad; yet he feels an attraction for Stella which he cannot place against a meaningful standard. Out of context as a poem by Sid-

ney, the final effect of the sonnet is that of a lover standing in bemused acceptance of the power of will; in context as a poem by
Astrophel, the final effect is that of a lover standing in resigned
confusion. Sidney had more knowledge of love than he allowed
Astrophel.

That he knew also more about philosophy is apparent in a poem
developed in a similar manner, but one that is radically different
in its final effect, namely, AS 71. Poetically, this sonnet is one of
Sidney's most daring poems. For thirteen lines he pays tribute to
a mature philosophy of love and life; then he adds a last line which
shows that the description has been only of a philosophy and
neither of love nor life. The poem is great because the first thirteen
lines are not undercut by the fourteenth; instead, they are forced
into a larger context; they are shown to be a model of life, not
life. Platonism, like Cupid in the previous poem, "An image is,
which for our selves we carve":[3]

> Who will in fairest booke of Nature know,
>> How Vertue may best lodg'd in beautie be,
>> Let him but learne of *Love* to reade in thee,
> *Stella,* those faire lines, which true goodnesse show.
> There shall he find all vices' overthrow,
>> Not by rude force, but sweetest soveraigntie
>> Of reason, from whose light those night-birds flie;
> That inward sunne in thine eyes shineth so.
>> And not content to be Perfection's heire
> Thy selfe, doest strive all minds that way to move,
> Who marke in thee what is in thee most faire.
> So while thy beautie drawes the heart to love,
>> As fast thy Vertue bends that love to good:
>> But ah, Desire still cries, 'give me some food.'

The modulations of voice in the first quatrain are calm and
thoughtful. After two lines of dependent clauses within which
meter and rhythm move along together, the main clause is introduced at the beginning of the third by a metrical substitution which
reinforces the syntactical and rhetorical movement, and is concluded in line four in a dramatic use of rising rhythm after the
opening trochee, "Stella," which, coming in apposition to the last
strong beat "thee" of line 3, gives the close of the quatrain a coda
effect.

After this introduction, the development follows in logical manner, the rythm of demonstration and discourse being indicated by the use of trochees introducing lines five, six, and eight, but avoiding a staccato effect by having line six run on into line seven. The personifications are not startling, as is fitting; for they suggest a typical microcosm-macrocosm metaphor, tinged with Platonism.

This Platonic note comes to the surface in the third quatrain when Stella is called "Perfection's heire," suggesting both that she is an earthly descendent of the good and beautiful, and that she will also inherit the good and beautiful (which is developed in lines ten through thirteen, in full accord with Neo-Platonic doctrine as set forth in works such as *The Courtier*). The calm and straight-forward nature of these lines is couched in absolutely regular iambic pentameter.

As was the case in the earlier "Thou blind man's marke," the poem could end here and be a good poem. There has been no satire, no irony, not even a touch of mockery. All has been doctrinaire, and set forth as a discourse of reason. But the poem becomes great when, in the last line, it becomes an implied dialogue of will and reason, a dialogue made dramatic by the fact that Astrophel is caught in the middle; for it is he, not Desire, who says, "But ah," indicating "Yes, but;—O.K., to all this I assent; still—." The poem then concludes with the masterful statement "give me some food," daringly put into prose to further contrast with the poetry of pure philosophy.

The clause concludes the poem, but does not end it; the whole line is so strong and passionate in contrast to the evenness and reasonableness of all that has gone before that the effect is of starting a new poem in the reader's mind: he cannot help being forced to take each aspect of the poem and weigh it. The result is not the acceptance of one part and rejection of the other, but the acceptance of both; for, in the act of weighing, of gently tossing each up and down, there comes over the reader, as was Sidney's aim, the realization that life needs its philosophical constructs, but that they are ultimately images, metaphors, or models, not the thing itself, because life is dynamic; yet, because it is dynamic, life needs philosophy to curb, control, and direct the energies of biology. Desire still cries, "give me some food"; but Reason replies, "not too much," an implication planted by Sidney for the reader to infer: Astrophel is still puzzled.

So far I have not mentioned the story of Astrophel and Stella because it is the least important aspect of the sequence, one of convention which usefully provides a kind of unity. The story itself is vague, its details few; and, as Jack C. Stillinger has pointed out, it is also slightly contradictory. There is a slight narrative movement, but all the events are as predictable as the hero and heroine. Still, tradition has identified Stella as Lady Penelope Devereux Rich.

The most notorious timeserver in the self-seeking age of the Tudors was the weathercock Richard Rich (1496–1567), who rose to power throughout the troublesome times of Henry VIII, Edward, Mary, and Elizabeth by successively betraying those who helped him: More, Cromwell, Seymour, Somerset, Gardiner, and finally Northumberland. In fact, the day after Rich signed the papers which declared that Princess Mary was illegitimate and proclaimed Lady Jane Grey as the rightful queen, he pledged Mary his support; and, during her reign, he won himself an infamous spot in Foxe's *Book of Martyrs* as executor of the faithful —the man who rode to power as betrayer of More and as destroyer of the monasteries! But somehow Baron Rich was named in 1558 as one of the escorts to London for Princess Elizabeth.

Sidney knew his son Robert Lord Rich (1537–1581) as a traveling companion to Paris in 1572; and, when in 1581, the Earl of Leicester and his wife, the former Countess of Essex, sought Richard Rich's grandson, the young Robert Rich, fresh inheritor of the family title and vast wealth, as the husband for Penelope Devereux, Sidney might well have blushed—but not out of any feeling for Penelope, only from family shame.

As Ringler has observed, Sidney probably did not meet Penelope until she came to court with her guardian, his Aunt Catherine, the Countess of Huntington, who was the sister of Leicester and Lady Mary. After Sidney got to know the proud, vivacious sister of his friend Robert, second Earl of Essex, the marriage seemed to have struck him as pathetically amusing, if his attitudes toward the Rich family and to the marriage appear in two sonnets, 24 and 37, of the *Astrophel and Stella* sequence:

> Rich fooles there be, whose base and filthy hart
> Lies hatching still the goods wherein they flow:
> And damning their owne selves to *Tantal's* smart,

Wealth breeding want, more blist, more wretched grow.
   Yet to those fooles heav'n such wit doth impart,
As what their hands do hold, their heads do know,
And knowing, love, and loving, lay apart
As sacred things, far from all daunger's show.
   But that rich foole, who by blind Fortune's lot
The richest gemme of Love and life enjoyes,
And can with foule abuse such beauties blot;
Let him, deprived of sweet but unfelt joyes,
   (Exil'd for ay from those high treasures, which
   He knowes not) grow in only follie rich.

*   *   *   *   *

My mouth doth water, and my breast doth swell,
   My tongue doth itch, my thoughts in labour be:
   Listen then Lordings with good eare to me,
For of my life I must a riddle tell.
Towardes *Aurora's* Court a Nymph doth dwell,
   Rich in all beauties which man's eye can see:
   Beauties so farre from reach of words, that we
Abase her praise, saying she doth excell:
   Rich in the treasure of deserv'd renowne,
Rich in the riches of a royall hart,
Rich in those gifts which give th'eternall crowne;
Who though most rich in these and everie part,
   Which make the patents of true wordly blisse,
   Hath no misfortune, but that Rich she is.

Although the name Stella appears in neither of these poems, the allusion to Lady Rich in the second seems clear, so clear that the surpression of it in the unauthorized edition of the sonnets of 1591 led Sir John Harrington in the 1590s, Matthew Gwinne in 1603, and Thomas Campion in 1619 to the conclusion that Stella must equal Penelope. But it was not they who went on to suggest a heartbreaking affair for Sidney; that elaboration was the work of biographers in the nineteenth and twentieth centuries.

That these three are the only Elizabethans who identified Stella as Penelope, that Spenser and Lodowick Bryskett both identified Stella as Frances Sidney, and that none other of the countless poets who wrote of Sidney or dedicated poems to both Lady Rich and to Frances (after 1590, the Countess of Essex) made an attempt at identification are potent facts which tend to overthrow the probability of any Penelope-Philip affair, especially the *kind* of affair posited by romantic biographers.[4]

The emphasis on *kind* is important; for, even if they did have an affair before, after, or before *and* after Penelope's marriage— she was neither an eager bride nor a chaste wife—given the temperaments of both Penelope and Philip, it could not have been the affair of popular accounts. Furthermore, *even if*—in contradiction to all we know in general from poets of all times concerning the poetic process and all we know in special concerning the writing of Renaissance poetry—*even if Astrophel and Stella,* which was freely circulated within the London literary circle, is autobiographical, the affair, whether with Penelope or whomsoever, was not very serious; for the prevalent tone of the poems, as Stillinger has pointed out, "is one of wit, urbanity, sophistication, and plain good humor" (634). These are exactly the qualities of Sidney and his literary ethos, and they are seen in all his works from *The Lady of May* of 1578 through the *New Arcadia* of 1584.

Still, in keeping with convention, *Astrophel and Stella* tells a story, such as it is. Astrophel sees Stella, slowly falls in love, tries to communicate his love, finally does, only to discover that she is, or just has been, married, which serves to increase his agony and her standoffishness—all typical of courtly romance, and affording Sidney the opportunity to display Astrophel in all the expected poses of the Petrarchan lover. The poems, and even songs, simply do not mesh together into a tightly knit drama. The climax of the story comes when Astrophel steals a kiss while Stella is sleeping, but the fact casually is slipped in, used in a variety of poems, and then dropped. In fact, the act takes place not in a sonnet, but in the "Second Song" between Sonnets 72 and 73.

Even after close examination, nothing can be found in Sonnet 71, "Who will in fairest booke of Nature," that is primarily important to a narrative. Sonnet 72 is a companion piece, a farewell to Desire:

> But thou Desire, because thou wouldst have all,
> Now banished art, but yet alas how shall?

Then follows the song in which Astrophel wakes Stella with a stolen kiss. Sonnet 73, following, says that she is angry; but Astrophel handles the matter with such comic delight that he can conclude

"That Anger' selfe I needs must kisse again." We find here no rapture—delight and desire—but no rapture. And this incident is followed by Sonnet 74, another poem having more to do with poetry than love. Sonnet 75 has nothing to do with Stella; Sonnets 76 and 77 are lip-smacking hexameter poems which make it clear that Astrophel wants to go to bed with Stella. And so the "story" goes on, until Astrophel is rejected outright, and the sequence ends in Sonnet 108 with Astrophel in the conventional dejected-rejected pose of the Petrarchan lover:

> When sorrow (using mine owne fier's might)
>   Melts downe his lead into my boyling brest,
>   Through that darke fornace to my hart opprest,
> There shines a joy from thee my only light;
> But soon as thought of thee breeds my delight,
>   And my yong soule flutters to thee his nest,
>   Most rude dispaire my daily unbidden guest,
> Clips streight my wings, streight wraps me in his night,
>   And makes me then bow downe my head, and say,
> Ah what doth *Phoebus'* gold that wretch availe,
> Whom iron doores do keepe from use of day?
> So strangely (alas) thy works in me prevaile,
> That in my woes for thee thou art my joy,
> And in my joyes for thee my only annoy.

Because Sidney forced himself in early poems to try all kinds of line and stanza patterns, he easily mastered the sonnet form. At the same time, he also discovered the fact that English poetry could have a formal basis and a natural flow. Thus, when he turned to "old *Petrarch's* long disceased woes," he had through exercise brought his art to a state of readiness which permitted him to imitate the master in the full Elizabethan sense. Using Invention, he created his persona and near-ego, Astrophel, whom he then put through the established Disposition of a Petrarchan sequence. And his use of Elocution, Memory, and Utterance brought out the *engergia,* or "inward tuch." We are right when we say that we hear Sidney in *Astrophel and Stella,* but we hear him *through* Astrophel not *as* him. We are free, of course, to listen only for Astrophel; but, if we do, we miss a mass of energy and a variety of touches.

Astrophel and Stella is one of the world's great collections of lyric poetry.

CHAPTER 6

New Arcadia

WHEN Sidney introduced Musidorus and Pyrocles in Book I of the *Old Arcadia*, he presented in outline their royal background and said that their visit to Arcadia was merely an interlude amid heroic endeavors, which would not be of present concern. Indeed, he said, "what befell unto them, what valyant actes they did, passing, (in one yeares space) throughe the lesser *Asia, Syria* and *Egipt,* how many Ladyes they defended from wronges, and disinherited persons restored to theyre Righte, yt ys a worcke for a higher style then myne" (IV, 8). Such a work is the *New Arcadia,* started possibly in late 1582 or early 1583, and left incomplete in 1584, but published in an edited form in 1590.

The last phrase quoted above can be interpreted in two ways: it means either "a work which would have to be written in a style more elevated than my style of writing" or "a work more elevated than my work." Although either interpretation fits the context, what is important is that the speaker is not Sidney but the narrator of the *Old Arcadia,* as his voice was presented in Book I of that work, that of a witty observer and presenter of a romantic comedy. And I place the emphasis on Book I for two reasons: first, a marked characteristic of the *Old Arcadia,* as we have seen, is the gradual impersonalization of the narrator so that by Book V his special voice has all but disappeared; and second, too often the difference between the *Old Arcadia* and the *New* is said to be a difference in Sidney's style. The difference, however, is of a larger kind.

Kenneth Muir has said that it cannot be "seriously maintained that the style of the old *Arcadia* is superior to that of the new." He then makes "a typical comparison" between the two versions, and he concludes that "the revised one is superior in several ways" (15–16). Although he does not give the location of his sources, they do in fact come from the two versions; but what Muir failed to see is that the second passage which he quotes is not a revision of the first passage, but a verbatim (except for one pluralization and one word change) repetition in the *New* of a passage which occurs in the *Old* merely seven pages after the first passage which he quotes from the *Old*. The point is that Sidney's style did not change; instead, he changed the mode from comic to heroic. As Muir has unwittingly demonstrated, Sidney could write heroically in the *Old*, as we have seen especially in the examination of Book V. When he undertook to recast the *Old* into the *New*, he disposed of his comic molds, and prepared heroic ones.

I   *"Et in Arcadia ego"*

To grasp this essential difference is to understand that the real change is in one of purpose, as Kenneth Myrick has demonstrably proved, with the result that the attitudes which inform and the tones which result in the *New Arcadia* are initially and finally different in kind from those of the *Old*. This change in attitude is obvious from the outset, not just in the epic's opening *in medias res,* but in the actual opening dialogue between the shepherds Strephon and Claius. This pair of friends had appeared in the eclogues of the *Old Arcadia,* having sung, notably, "Yee Gote-heard Gods" in the fourth set; and Sidney mentioned them, among others, in his epilogue as being subjects whom someone else might wish to pursue in some other work. The plan for the *New Arcadia* had not been developed at that time because some characters were mentioned who do not (and could not) appear in this fragment. But Sidney had kept these shepherds in mind, as he had Philisides; for, as Ringler has shown, he wrote poems for them between work on the two prose pieces; and although he did not include their songs in his revision, his sister did put them into her own expanded version, the *Arcadia* of 1593.

Even though Strephon and Claius appear only in the opening scenes and sing no songs, their function is clear: they are a chorus used to reveal what Arcadia is and is not. Their opening dialogue is introduced by the narrator, who sets the time as spring: "*It was in the time* that the earth begins to put on her new aparrel against the approach of her lover, and that the Sun running a most even course becums an indifferent arbiter betweene the night and the day" (I, 5). When the reader discovers that both the shepherds have been in love with the same woman without being rivals, that

she departed for Cythera, that her name is Urania, and that she
has fully led them out of their dark selves into a learned state—
"hath not shee throwne reason upon our desires, and, as it were
given eyes unto *Cupid*?" (I, 8)—the typology is manifest. The
beginning of spring suggests the beginning of life; the beginning
of life was the result of the coming together of Uranus and Tellus
Mater, whose daughter was Aphrodite Ourania or the Celestial
Venus, here the Urania who has departed for her "home" on
Cythera, the traditional birthplace of Aphrodite. Thus the world
of Arcadia is the fallen world, but one that is *informed*. That is,
Venus has come to earth, involving it with purpose, and has left;
therefore, worship of Venus is tribute to the source and end of
life at the same time that it is the means of coming to understand
the source and end.

Urania, personifying the three aspects of Venus, has allowed
her beauty to attract these humble men in order to elevate them
and inspire them with a vision of wholeness. In her role as Venus
the daughter of Jove, she has operated in their senses; as Venus
the daughter of Saturn, she has operated in their reason; and as
Venus daughter of Uranus, she has operated in their soul, their
link to heaven. But she has gone: "woe is me, yonder, yonder, did
she put her foote into the boate, at that instant as it were deviding
her heavenly beautie, betweene the Earth and the Sea" (I, 6).
This reversal of the usual portrayal of the birth of Venus is appropriate, for it suggests that the world left behind has become a
fallen one.

Complementing this thematic suggestion, the story itself opens
with the washing up on shore of Musidorus who has miraculously
escaped the Ship of Death. This emblem is further enriched by the
fact that he comes ashore not in Arcadia (which, as Ringler has
pointed out, Sidney discovered after writing the *Old Arcadia* would
have been impossible) but in Laconia, a land rife with civil war.
Moreover, he and Pyrocles are not simply on their way home at
the time of the accident but are headed for Arcadia as an extension of their heroic endeavors, reports of which are woven into
the narrative of Book I and, especially, Book II.

By his opening, then, Sidney emphasizes the fact that the
Arcadia of this work is not the same as that of the previous one.
To be sure, once Musidorus and his two guides have crossed the

border, one of the first sights is Keatsian, "a shepheards boy piping, as though he should never be old" (I, 13); but essentially Arcadia is merely another country of the Peloponnesus, only one blessed "with peace, and (the childe of peace) good husbandrie" (I, 14). By the end of Book II and for all of Book III, however, civil war rages in Arcadia; and in Book I, a war is waged against strife-torn Laconia in order to save Clitophon, the son of Kalendar, (and incidentally in order to reunite Musidorus and Pyrocles). Some twenty years before anyone else, Sidney records the fact that death too dwells in Arcadia.[1]

II *Books I and II, Variety of Style and Voice*

Reinforcing this opening up of the world of the new book are the removal of the revelation of the oracle from the very beginning of Book I to the end of Book II (by which time all past events have been reported) and the shift away from a personalized narrator to an impersonal one—one who does not so much report as record, for Sidney uses here a constantly shifting "point of view," as that term has come to be used in modern criticism. Dialogue abounds; and, when narrative background is needed and stories occur, they are presented by characters. Because of these facts, again, to talk about the "style" of the *New Arcadia* as if it were of a piece is to be unaware of the variety of styles that Sidney interposes; for what we have seen as characteristic of Sidney's from *The Lady of May* through *Astrophel and Stella* is his experimenting with "voice."

As Zandvoort and Myrick have demonstrated, Sidney reused most of the material of Books I and II of the *Old Arcadia* in his expansion; but, when these old parts are placed in the mouths of a number of different characters and amid a wealth of new action, the old tones are muted and transmuted. For example, what had been the opening description of Arcadia by the narrator is now given to Kalendar (I, 19), to whose home the shepherds take Musidorus. Through the description of his well-appointed house and "Elizabethan" gardens we discover that Kalendar is a man of taste, some wealth, and of a settled disposition. When he talks, we know that he is wise and judicious, but old enough to observe life with humor, even did he not provide his own self-characterization:

And now you know as much as my self: wherin if I have held you over long, lay hardly the fault upon my olde age, which in the very disposition of it is talkative: whether it be (said he smiling) that nature loves to exercise that part most, which is least decayed, and that is our tongue: or, that knowledge being the only thing wherof we poore old men can brag, we cannot make it knowen but by utterance: or, that mankinde by all meanes seeking to eternize himselfe so much the more, as he is neere his end, dooth it not only by the children that come of him, but by speeches and writings recommended to the memorie of hearers and readers. (I, 27)

Kalendar's description of Basilius has been honest, yet sufficiently guarded to be respectful: "But to be plaine with you, he excels in nothing so much, as in the zealous love of his people, wherein he doth not only passe al his owne fore-goers, but as I thinke al the princes living. Wherof the cause is, that though he exceed not in the vertues which get admiration; as depth of wisdome, height of courage and largenesse of magnificence, yet is hee notable in those whiche stirre affection, as trueth of worde, meekenesse, courtesie, mercifulnesse, and liberalitie" (I, 19).

And Kalendar went on to depict accurately Gynecia, a woman "of notable beautie, as by her picture you see: a woman of great wit, and in truth of more princely vertues, then her husband: of most unspotted chastitie, but of so working a minde, and so vehement spirits, as a man may say, it was happie shee tooke a good course: for otherwise it would have beene terrible" (I, 19–20). When he describes the princesses he does so without irony; but he carefully differentiates their personalities. When he gets to Dametas, Miso, and Mopsa, however, his sense of humor is fully revealed. In fact, here, as in the description of Arcadia, Sidney gives Kalendar the description of Miso earlier used by the narrator of the *Old Arcadia* (see above, p. 75). He then goes on to quote the fourteener sonnet about Mopsa (see above, p. 89), in this version now attributed to "a pleasant fellow of my acquaintance," thereby allowing the comic effects to reverberate in context as a joke shared by him and Musidorus and not out of context as one for the narrator and his lady friends, as had been the case in the earlier work.

After Kalendar and Musidorus return from their stroll around the grounds, the point of view shifts when Kalendar retires to his room in grief over the news that his son Clitophon has been captured by the rebelling Helots of Laconia; and Musidorus is given occasion to ask the steward of the house for more details about persons and events. The steward is, however, a long time in giving his answers because he is a kind of forerunner of Polonius: diplomatic, gossipy, guarded, and so highly self-conscious about his manner of speaking that it becomes periodic and involuted:

but I say for my part, I thinke no man for valour of minde, and habilitie of bodie to bee preferred, if equalled to *Argalus;* and yet so valiant as he never durst doo any bodie injurie: in behaviour some will say ever sadde, surely sober, and somewhat given to musing, but never uncourteous; his worde ever ledde by his thought, and followed by his deede; rather liberall then magnificent, though the one wanted not, and the other had ever good choise of the receiver: in summe (for I perceive I shall easily take a great draught of his praises, whom both I and all this countrie love so well) such a man was (and I hope is) *Argalus,* as hardly the nicest eye can finde a spot in, if the over-vehement constancie of yet spotles affection, may not in harde wrested constructions be counted a spot: which in this manner began that worke in him, which hath made bothe him, and it selfe in him, over all this country famous. My maisters sonne *Clitophon* (whose losse gives the cause to this discourse, and yet gives me cause to beginne with *Argalus,* since his losse proceedes from *Argalus*) beyng a young Gentleman, as of great birth (being our kings sisters sonne) so truely of good nature, and one that can see good and love it, haunted more the companie of this worthie *Argalus,* then of any, *etc.* (I, 31)

The quotation is long, but still incomplete; for the steward revels in the opportunity to tell all. But he really is more interested in his own words than in what he says. Talking of Argalus's beloved, Parthenia, he says, "that which made her fairenesse much the fayrer, was, that it was but a faire embassadour of a most faire minde, full of wit, and a wit which delighted more to judge it selfe, then to showe it selfe: her speach being as rare as pretious; her silence without sullennesse; her modestie without affectation; her shamefastnes without ignorance: in summe, one, that to praise well, *one must first set downe with himselfe, what it is to be excellent:* for so she is" (I, 32). And the phrase I have emphasized gives him away: he has been to grammar school and knows the proper use of a common-place book. Furthermore, in concluding the first part of the story of Argalus and Parthenia, he states, "Truely Sir, a very good Orator might have a fayre field to use eloquence in, if he did only repeate [Argalus's] lamentable, and truely affectionated speeches" (I, 35).

Whereas Kalendar's art is hidden in his speech and the steward's shows, Mopsa in hers is simply artless. When it falls to her lot in Book II to tell a story, she begins:

In time past (sayd she) there was a King, the mightiest man in all his country, that had by his wife, the fairest daughter that ever did eate pappe. Now this King did keepe a great house, that every body might come and take their meat freely. So one day, as his daughter was sitting in her window, playing upon a harpe, as sweete as any Rose; and combing her head with a combe all of precious stones, there came in a Knight into the court, upon a goodly horse, one haire of gold, & the other of silver; *and so* the Knight casting up his eyes to the window, did fall into such love with her, that he grew not worth the bread he eate; till many a sorry day going over his head, with Dayly Diligence and Grisly Grones, he wan her affection, so that they agreed to run away togither. *And so in May, when all true hartes rejoyce, . . . And so . . . , And then . . . , And so . . ."* (I, 241)

But as was Chaucer in telling the tale of Sir Thopas, she is interrupted before she can finish her tale.

Mopsa's character is carried over from the *Old Arcadia,* as are her parents, and the other central figures: Basilius (now a Prince), Gynecia, their daughters, and the two princes. Dametas and his family, and Basilius and his wife, however, do not loom so large because their roles are not expanded: hence, here they must compete for attention because of the many additions of people both in person and in report. The first kind of added characters, such as Kalendar and his steward, take on individuality; and the second kind, because they are reported, serve to reveal the personalities of those who tell their stories.

Major examples of the first kind are Cecropia and Amphialus who dominate Book III, but who are central throughout all three books. Cecropia is responsible for the bear and lion at the end of Book I (an accident in the *Old*), the rebellion in Book II (a spontaneous riot in the *Old*), and is cause of the siege in Book III because she planned the capture of Philoclea and Pamela (as well as Pyrocles, now disguised as Zelmane). Her attempts to seduce the young ladies are so masterful that they point up all the more the virtue of the princesses. Playing her role of loving aunt, she fills her address to Philoclea with "sweet neece," "my deare neece," (I, 377–78) but all to no avail. When rebuffed, she explodes and is the opposite of all that she pretends to be, thus revealing the breadth of her personality.

Such a person has the fitting son in Amphialus, a Coriolanus figure in that he is warlike and mother-dominated, but who is a much more appealing person—one almost fated to do the wrong thing when he wants to do well. In Book I, we find that he has unwittingly killed his best friend, Philoxenus (whose father in turn dies of a broken heart); he is loved by Helena, beautiful Queen of Corinth, but in Book II falls in love with Philoclea when he comes upon her bathing; in that scene he is wounded by Pyrocles, but he thinks he has succumbed to a woman's blade because Pyrocles is disguised as an Amazon; in Book III he knows he should free the ladies, but his will is not controlled by his reason; and time after time he wounds or kills in defense of his chivalric honor, only to fall deeper into despair over the havoc and chaos he is causing. Finally, he attempts suicide after the deaths of Parthenia and his mother.

The other kind of added character, the reported, serves to expand the personalities of the central lovers, mainly in Book II. But these four lovers play larger roles in the *New Arcadia* than they had in the *Old*: in Book I, Pyrocles and Musidorus (along with Argalus) restore temporary order in Laconia, Musidorus gets involved with Helena because he has assumed Amphialus's discarded armor, and both take part in the elaborate pageantry of Phalantus's tournament. Interspersed with these new events are the old, so that Pyrocles still falls in love with Philoclea's picture and goes to the retreat in disguise; Musidorus falls in love with Pamela and, as a shepherd, joins his friend; and the same comic-romantic situation concludes the Book. But the context has been so expanded that the retreat is not the center of focus; it becomes merely another place among many.

The retreat might have received more emphasis if Sidney had provided a set of eclogues between Books I and II, but he did not, as Greville's important prefatory note to the *New Arcadia* makes clear: "*If any defect be found in the Eclogues, which although*

*they were of Sir Phillip Sidneis writing, yet were they not perused
by him, but left till the worke had bene finished, that then choise
should have bene made, which should have bene taken, and in
what manner brought in. At this time they have bene chosen and
disposed as the over-seer thought best"* (I, 4).

To be sure, Book I ends with the statement that the characters
were going to witness pastoral entertainment, and Book II opens
saying that they had. But the *New Arcadia* as Sidney left it, as
Ringler has pointed out, should be read without the eclogues put
in by Greville and certainly without the eclogues as restored and
expanded by the Countess of Pembroke. In fact, of the twenty-six
poems retained in the *New,* fifteen are direct carry-overs within
the retained materials of the *Old Arcadia* double love story: the
fourteener description of Mopsa; various laments by Pyrocles,
Musidorus, Philoclea, Gynecia, and Basilius; and Dametas's song
of triumph and Basilius's Hymn to Apollo both at the end of
Book II. As for the remaining ones, those of narrative value are
the slightly changed Oracle now at the end of Book II, and the
lament of Plangus reported by Basilius, taken from the old second
eclogues. Four other eclogue poems are interwoven into the narrative, as is CS 3; but each of these, like the laments, is simply
there for tonal effect; they are good but not great. Two "new"
poems were introduced, one a stanza recollected by Pyrocles from
a longer song once sung by Philisides, and the other the one-line
hexameter of Dametas. The twenty-sixth poem is from the *Old*
(OA 62), the catalogue poem which passed through Pyrocles's
mind as he watched Philoclea tossing in her sleep at the end of
Book III. There the context was comic, but now it is much more
serious and sensuous; for Zelmane-Pyrocles makes it up as he
sings aloud to his lute watching the sisters bathing in the stream
in Book II. That Sidney liked the poem is demonstrated by the
many corrections and additions he made in it between various
transcriptions of the *Old Arcadia,* as Ringler has shown; and the
fact is reinforced by his introduction to it here:

In somuch that taking up the Lute, her wit began to be with a divine
furie inspired; her voice would in so beloved an occasion second her
wit; her hands accorded the Lutes musicke to the voice; her panting
hart daunced to the musicke; while I thinke her feete did beate the
time; while her bodie was the roome where it should be celebrated;

her soule the Queene which shoulde be delighted. And so togither went the utterance and the invention, that one might judge, it was *Philocleas* beautie which did speedily write it in her eyes; or the sense thereof, which did word by word endite it in her minde, whereto she (but as an organ) did onely lend utterance. (I, 218)

Book II, like Book I, is constructed by interspersing new events with old, but the new events are reported; hence Book II seemingly contains more "action" than the other two, even Book III, but is actually more static. These reports (except for Mopsa's interrupted story, they are basically expansions of Histor's accounts of the princes in the eclogues of the *Old*) show the heroic achievements of the two princes, just as had the added combats in Book I. The purpose of these events is stated outright by Musidorus: the two princes had set out "privately to seeke exercises of their vertue; thinking it not so worthy, to be brought to heroycall effects by fortune, or necessitie (like *Ulysses* and *Aeneas*) as by ones owne choice, and working" (I, 206). But in addition to the heroic value of the stories, we have their contribution to the overall motif of love that unites all three books of the *New,* as Walter Davis in a generally misleading book has brilliantly shown. The world of the *New Arcadia* is a fallen one; Venus (Urania) has departed and the discords of love abound. We are tempted to look ahead to Shakespeare's *Venus and Adonis* with its final prophecy of discord between the sexes and its final action:

> Thus weary of the world away she hies,
> And yokes her silver doves; by whose swift aid
> Their mistress, mounted, through the empty skies
> In her light chariot quickly is conveyed;
>> Holding their course to Phaphos where their queen
>> Means to immuse herself and not be seen.

Even the noble love of Argalus and Parthenia, which was reported in Book I, comes to a disastrous end in Book III, thus appropriately framing Book II.

Within Book II, the central reported episode is that of Plangus and Queen Erona who, having destroyed all the images of love in her kingdom, immediately fell in love with Anti-philus. Significantly, her story is told mainly by Philoclea and Pamela; for

Erona, as Danby has suggested, is the woman-in-love figure most removed from the two princesses, representing, as she does, along with her lover, the destructive, overly passionate side of love. That Philoclea and Pamela should tell her story (as reported to them by Plangus who passed through Arcadia in search of the two princes, for whom Erona in the depth of her plight has sent) is appropriate because the story highlights not only the positive womanly virtues of the princesses but also suggests the danger that lies ahead if those virtues are not controlled and developed to womanly fulfillment. Thus, the tales bearing on love told by the princesses have a positive and ironic side, just as do the tales mainly bearing on duty told by the princes.

Furthermore, the tragedy of Erona and Plangus, coming as it does in the middle of Book II (after Musidorus has told the tales of the King of Phrygia, King Pontus, and the King of Paphlagonia —often cited as the model for Shakespeare's Gloucester in *King Lear*—and after the bathing episode, complete with the wounding of Amphialus) acts both as a counterweight to the comedy of love played in the retreat and as a complement to the tragedy of Amphialus in Book III.

Before the new action of Book III, however, Pyrocles brings the *New Arcadia* "up to date," ending Book II by telling the stories of Pamphilus, Chremes, Andromana, and Plexirtus, at which point the *Old Arcadia* thread is picked up again with the outbreak of the rebellion, which is again quelled by Pyrocles-Zelmane, first by sword:

Yet among the rebels there was a dapper fellowe, a tayler by occupation, who fetching his courage onelie from their going back, began to bow his knees, & very fencer-like to draw neere to *Zelmane.* But as he came within her distance, turning his swerd very nicely about his crown, *Basilius,* with a side blow, strake of his nose. He (being a suiter to a seimsters daughter, and therfore not a little grieved for such a disgrace) stouped downe, because he had hard, that if it were fresh put to, it would cleave on againe. But as his hand was on the grounde to bring his nose to his head, *Zelmane* with a blow, sent his head to his nose. That saw a butcher, a butcherlie chuffe indeed (who that day was sworn brother to him in a cup of wine) & lifted up a great leaver, calling *Zelmane* all the vile names of a butcherly eloquence. But she (letting slippe the blowe of the leaver) hitte him so surely on the side of his face, that she lefte nothing but the nether jawe, where the tongue still wagged, as willing to say more, if his masters remembrance had served. O (said a miller that was halfe dronke) see the lucke of a good fellow. (I, 312)

But then finally by her eloquence.

The Book thus ends generally in accord with the *Old:* Dametas claims credit for the victory, and Basilius is even more in love with Zelmane-Pyrocles, thinks the oracle is fulfilled, reveals it, and sings a hymn of thanksgiving to Apollo. Unlike the *Old,* however, in the *New* the details of the oracle have not been told, thus some suspense has been maintained from Book I; and here Cecropia is behind the rebels, thus linking Book II to Book III. The Book closes with the nobles going off to watch pastorals, but not before Basilius, fittingly, tells the rest of the story of Plangus, who has been advised by Basilius to seek Evarchus.

III   *The Broken Book*

Unlike the previous books, Book III is linear and completely new: it starts with the capture of the two princesses and Zelmane-Pyrocles by Cecropia in order to soothe her son Amphialus; and it is developed by the siege, by the various individual challenges made of Amphialus, and by the comic interlude of Dametas and Clineas, which occurs after the death of Argalus and before the death of Parthenia.

The deaths of these two mark the ebb of chivalry in the work; but, ironically, no book in the *Old* or in the *New Arcadia* is so filled with the ceremonies and color of knightly tournament. But, as the encounters become more intense and complicated and as the dress and attendance of Amphialus and his challengers become more elaborate, the wounds and killings become harsher and more brutal. The action is quite like that of Book VI of *The Fairie Queene* before the interlude in Acidale. In both books, the world of chivalry is an acting out of the emblem which Shakespeare interjected at the end of *Troilus and Cressida,* when Hector pursues a Greek accoutered in shining armor, only to discover, upon overtaking his mark and killing him, a rottenness within: "Most putrefied core, so fair without, Thy goodly armor thus hath cost thy life" (V, viii, 1–2). And the parallel carries farther: just as the decadence of chivalry in *Troilus and Cressida* is given contrasting emphasis through the positive values expounded by Hector in arguing from the laws of Nature and of Nations, and by Ulysses in his defense of order, so also Pamela's refutation of Cecropia's epicurean atheism contrasts with, and hence emphasizes, the nature of the action. Her invocation of divine order in "universall Nature" (I, 406–10) is in detail and design similar to that part of Du Mornay which Sidney translated.

With the entrance of Anaxius, who comes in support of Amphialus, all pretensions to glamor and grandeur are dispelled. Bent on rape and rapine, "not recking law of armes, nor use of chivalrie" (I, 462), he is an inversion of all that a knight should be: "so proud, as he could not abstaine from a *Thraso*-like boasting, and yet (so unluckie a lodging his vertues had gotten) he would never boast more then he would accomplish: falsly accounting an unflexible anger, a couragious constancie: esteeming feare, and astonishment, righter causes of admiration, then Love and Honour" (I, 439). Pyrocles-Zelmane puts the final stamp on the character and behavior of Anaxius:

And therefore, as a hangman, I say, thou art unworthy to be counted a Knight, or to be admitted into the companie of Knights. Neither for what, I say, will I alleadge other reasons, of wisdome, or justice, to proove my speech, because I know thou doost disdaine to be tied to their rules: but even in thine owne vertue (whereof thou so much gloriest) I will make my triall: and therefore defie thee, by the death of one of us two, to prove, or disprove these reproaches. Choose thee what armes thou likest, I onely demaund, that these Ladies (whom I defend) may in liberty see the combat. (I, 505)

The description of their fight is as real, extended, and detailed as any in Sidney; but it is cut off in the midst of a sentence.

How Sidney might have developed his narrative is unknown. Certainly from the nature of the revision of the oracle, the two princes at the final trial would have been charged with conspiracy to murder Basilius, not with rape and royal abduction:

Thy elder care shall from thy carefull face
By princely meane be stolne, and yet not lost.
Thy yonger shall with Natures blisse embrace
An uncouth love, which Nature hateth most.
Both they themselves unto such two shall wed,
Who at thy beer, as at a barre, shall plead;

Why thee (a living man) they had made dead.
In thy owne seate a forraine state shall sit.
And ere that all these blowes thy head doo hit,
Thou, with thy wife, adultry shall commit. (I, 327)

Such a conclusion would have removed, as Ringler has observed, the awkwardness of the pardon of the princes, for the only charges against them pertain to murder, not attempted rape and abduction of an heir apparent. With Ringler's revelation of how the account of Evarchus's arrival in Arcadia on his way to help Erona in Book V of the 1593 *Arcadia* dovetails with the existing geographical and plot revisions of the *New Arcadia* of 1590, there lies the additional possibility that, in Sidney's notes concerning a revision of the *Old Arcadia,* Plangus might have reappeared in person to remind the reader of the princes' one unfulfilled quest: the freeing of Queen Erona (that Venus figure in the work farthest removed from Urania). But the unfinished nature of Book III—the castle of Amphialus, for example, is first placed on a rock island in the middle of the lake, then it is described as backing on the lake, and finally it is said to be the key to the defense of a walled town, outside of which is the lake and the island on which the last individual trials take place—and the fact that by Book III Sidney had dropped completely the narrative of the *Old Arcadia* make us wonder whether he had so departed from his original plan of revision and expansion that he could no longer return to it. Indeed, he may even have questioned the efficacy of his esthetic reliance on "Art, Imitation, and Exercise."

IV   *A New Kind of Imitation*

A great writer is self-consciously unselfconscious—"Negative Capability" was Keats's rough-hewn formulation; Eliot's, "an escape from personality"—and much of Sidney, more of Spenser, and most of Shakespeare can be called "great" through application of this truism. But in *form,* because of the pervasive influence of the doctrine of rhetorical imitation, most Elizabethan literary art is *un*selfconsciously *self*-conscious—which is one way of indicating that the Elizabethan, be he artist or of the audience, was not disturbed by the fact that his art was primarily traditional and patterned, that it proceeded from the known and established, that its *données* were immense and demanding.

In spite of this fact, most Elizabethan writing is vital simply because it remains close to life; it is, in a simultaneously valid sense, an imitation of the products of Dame Nature, as Sidney stated in the *Defence.* But this kind of self-conscious art could remain vital only so long as the artist believed feelingly and unselfconsciously that neither art nor nature was real. His soul, wit, imagination, or reason was real, and God was real; but the products of selfhood and God, art and nature, were not. For this reason, the major episodes in the *New Arcadia* are sacramental, not sentimental, even though set in the never-never land of knightly romance.

Art to Sidney was an imitation of human life which made comprehensive and comprehensible the qualities of humanity through its projection of human activity. Because the subject was man, the mode which allowed one to display the broadest range of qualities and the greatest sweeps of action yielded the highest art. It did not matter, therefore, that chivalry was literally dead, for the world of romance was the perfect model to exploit in literature, *as in a triumph at court,* to present the Renaissance ideal of life as service and fulfillment, through adherence to the obligations and demands of love and duty, in both the private and the public aspects of life. The world of romance is, nevertheless, unreal; and for that reason it is a self-conscious world. A great sixteenth-century artist such as Sidney through his *energia* and negative capability unreflectingly makes that world real to his reader; but, when the poet-writer experienced the fact that he had made that world real, he could no longer unselfconsciously work within circumscribed modes. Such was the recognition, I submit, experienced by Sidney as he neared the end of Book III of the *New Arcadia.*

The Lady of May and the *Old Arcadia* are fine examples of unselfconsciously created self-conscious art, the first being an elaborated form of Italian rustic comedy and the second being a prose pastoral-courtly-romance treated as if it were an academic five-act comedy. Kenneth Myrick and Marcus Goldman long ago conclusively demonstrated that, when Sidney took up his work on the *New Arcadia,* he had the generic and ethical ideals of the romance epic before him—the initial evidence is to be found in the tone and manner of the final book of the *Old Arcadia.* There the narrator's voice began to lose its special personality, a personality which Sidney completely writes out of the *New Arcadia,* where there is, instead, the shifting point of view of third-person description and narration, straight dialogue and indirect discourse, and even interior monologue. To be sure, the impress of Sidney is everywhere apparent, and here too there is an evolution of seriousness, but this time *in kinds of action.* This shift necessarily is accompanied by a movement away from the rural retreat of Basilius, first by means of the reported episodes, mainly in Book II, then in Book III, by the physical shift directly to the siege of Amphialus's castle.

Until Book III, and during the first challenges of the castle and the initial trials held on the island, the customs and ceremonies of chivalry served the ends of Sidney's art: the projection of courtly, human ideals. But, during the fight between Argalus and Amphialus, the description becomes forthrightly realistic. The periods are what have come to be called "Arcadian"; the moves, like Romeo's first kisses, are all by the book; and the antagonists behave as if they were fighting in front of Queen Elizabeth's "Fortress of Perfect Beauty." But here the forms of rhetoric, art, and life merge *self-consciously.* The frustrations, the fatigue, the hurts, the cuts, simply are real:

For *Amphialus* (following his fawning fortune) laid on so thicke upon *Argalus,* that his shield had almost fallen peece-meale to the earth, when *Argalus* comming in with his right foote, and something stowping to come under his armour, thrust him into the belly daungerously, and mortally it would have beene, but that with the blowe before, *Amphialus* had overthrowne himself so, as he fell side-warde down, and with falling saved himselfe from ruine. The sworde by that meanes slipping aside, and not pearcing more deepely, *Argalus* seeing him fall, threatning with voyce and sworde, bad him yeelde. But he striving without aunswere to rise, *Argalus* strake with all his might upon his head. But his hurte arme not able to maister so sounde a force, let the swoorde fall so, as *Amphialus,* though astonished with the blowe, could arise: which *Argalus* considering, ranne in to graspe with him, and so closed together; falling so to the ground. (I, 424)

Because this fight is fully experienced by the writer and the reader, the death of Argalus is not sacramental. Even less so is that of Parthenia, who comes dressed as the Knight of the Tombs to revenge the death of her husband. Their deaths, however, are not sentimental because the woe felt by Sidney is artistically sincere. His epitaph for them, in or out of context, is moving:

> His being was in her alone:
> And he not being, she was none.
>   They joi'd one joy, one griefe they griev'd,
>   One love they lov'd, one life they liv'd.
>   The hand was one, one was the sword
>   That did his death, hir death afford.
> As all the rest, so now the stone
> That tombes the two, is justly one.[2]

When Amphialus destroys his sword because "it was [not] worthie to serve the noble exercise of chivalrie" (I, 450), we can sense that Sidney is making a comment on a way of life, and, with the exception of his description of the encounter between Amphialus and Musidorus disguised as the Black Knight, the heart seems to have gone out of Sidney's writing just as he says the heart has gone out of Amphialus. Indeed, in this now completely fallen, tragic-comic world, the forced, stylized comedy of Basilius in love with Zelmane-Pyrocles that is carried over from the *Old Arcadia* is painfully, uncomfortably out of place. The dispirited description of the plots, counterplots, and devices within the castle seem to testify that Sidney realized as much; but the clinching proof is in the final, incomplete description of personal trial, the hand-to-hand struggle between Anaxius and Pyrocles still disguised as Zelmane.

Sidney knew that his manner of description by this stage of Book III had evolved to the exact depiction of moves, thoughts, sounds, and effects. He tellingly remarks: "The Irish greyhound, against the English mastiffe; the sword-fish, against the whale; the Rhinoceros, against the elephant, might be models, and but models, of this combat" (I, 517). *"And but models"* because "this combat" is unique, is real:

Thus spent they a great time, striving to doo, and with striving to doo, wearying themselves, more then with the very doing. *Anaxius* finding *Zelmane* so neere unto him, that with little motion he might reach her, knitting all his strength together, at that time mainly foyned at her face. But *Zelmane* strongly putting it by with her right hande sword, comming in with her left foote, and hande, woulde have given him a sharpe visitation to his right side, but that he was faine to leape away. Whereat ashamed, (as having never done so much before in his life)—(I, 519).

The pronoun "her" destroys the vigor, immediacy, and veracity, and Sidney seems to have quit writing in disgust.

V *"His End Was not Writing"*

The shock of this recognition seems to have killed Sidney's endeavors of art: he left no indication whatsoever that he intended to return to this revision. The notes which Greville mentioned in November, 1586, to Walsingham clearly refer to what Sidney wanted to amend in the *Old Arcadia;* because Greville had heard that Ponsonby wished to print "Sir philip sydneys old arcadia," he said that he had "a correction of that old one don 4 or 5 years since which he left in trust with me wherof ther is no more copies, & fitter to be printed then that first one which is so common, notwithstanding euen that to be amended by a direction sett doun vndre his own hand how & why."[3] To be sure, when Sidney started the *New Arcadia,* it was this never-revised version of the *Old* which he had in the back of his mind. But, as the existing three Books demonstrate, the *Old Arcadia* faded from his attention, so much so that Basilius's arrival on the scene in Book III must have—to paraphrase Robert Frost—surprised Sidney as much as it surprises the reader. Sidney seems to have left off because he discovered that his art could no longer be considered merely a courtly pastime, but was a mistress as serious and demanding as Elizabeth; and he chose the Queen—his discipline was to be the cause of England against Spain, first by defensively arming the Channel coast, then by planning global, diversionary strategy, and at last by direct confrontation in the Netherlands.

If Sidney had remained an artist, the logical step for him to have taken was to the novel proper. But such an observation is from the grandstand. Because nature for him was not yet real, he could not have made his art a literal imitation of nature—as much as Bacon might have welcomed the attempt. Perhaps here again we can see, as is being suggested more and more often, how much the great art of the Renaissance is suspended between two worlds: the Medieval and modern.

Not until the twentieth century, however, could such an obser-

vation be made with regard to Sidney because of the ironic effect
of one aspect of the loving supervision by the Countess of Pembroke of the publication of her brother's "collected works" in
1598. Because of her, the authority of the *Defence* of 1595 over
the *Apologie* of the same year is established; because of her, we
have a version of *Astrophel and Stella* vastly superior to the
unauthorized versions of 1591; because of her, the *Certaine Sonets*
and *The Lady of May* were not lost. But also because of her, the
world has celebrated an *Arcadia* that is not of Sidney's making,
but of hers. In 1593, when she reedited the Greville edition of the
New Arcadia of 1590, she completed it by adding the last three
books of the *Old Arcadia* taken from her own copy, but amended
in accordance with the "direction" left by Sidney; and this *Arcadia*
she reprinted in 1598.

While we can thank her for having preserved the materials
which allow us to claim Sidney as a major poet and writer, her
handling of the *Arcadia* is another matter. To be sure, we must
accept with C. S. Lewis the historical importance of her *Arcadia*
of 1593, for it is the version the world has long known and, based
on the number of reprints and editions, long loved. But in spite
of Walter Davis's claim that the 1593 version represents what
Sidney would have written had he lived, full appreciation of
Sidney's achievement in prose fiction can come only through a
detailed comparison, such as Zandervoort initiated and Myrick
attempted, of the *Old Arcadia* and the fragment known as the
New Arcadia. We must realize that we can no longer talk vaguely
about "Sidney's *Arcadia*," but must distinguish among three versions, the first two of which were lost to the public for three hundred years, but the third of which, even in its pieced-together form,
was sufficiently appealing to win Sidney a reputation as an important and influential writer of prose fiction along with his reputation
as distinguished poet and critic.

Epilogue

IN both his life and his art, Sir Philip Sidney was and is a central figure of the English Renaissance; his life was the realization of ideals expressed by Elyot and Hoby; his art was influential in three areas. Although too many previous studies have been content to focus on the life, or the criticism, or the poetry, or the fiction, such attention is just because Sidney was typed by his age as the perfect scholar-statesman-soldier, and he was a major practitioner in each genre. But Sidney never separated sharply his endeavors: they all were simply aspects of his way of life as an Elizabethan gentleman.

In preparation for such a life, his education, in school and out, was that of the courtier, so that while "Art, Imitation, and Exercise" was an academic program, it was for Sidney an ethic and also an esthetic consideration. Without "Exercise," such a guide to life and literature would have led to mere grace and formality. But Sidney was constantly engaged with life and was increasingly so by art, with the result that the integrity of the life became more and more apparent in the art. *Because of* "Art" and "Imitation," however, the art never became mere biography or expressionism.

Sidney did not achieve this balance at once, even though he achieved it rapidly; for the duration of his artistic production was relatively short—seven years at the very most. Beginning even in *The Lady of May,* there is an engaging quality, a certain energy which becomes even more noticeable in the course of the five Books of the *Old Arcadia.* The experiments in poetry led naturally to a kind of fullness and wholeness which possesses, and which I have called "voice." This voice reached poetic maturity in *Astrophel and Stella,* but it remains a voice not always fully appreciated because, through the romanticizing of biographers, the artistic voice of Sidney has too often been regarded as his personal voice.

The heroic nature of the *New Arcadia* does not so easily lend itself to this kind of misreading (although the heavy hands of allegorizers have fallen on the New Arcadia). Sidney here remained so in control, so kept his art, imitation, and exercise in balance that the work is thoroughly engaging: the impress of the artist is everywhere apparent, but nowhere obtrusive. Paradoxically, the New Arcadia became so completely independent, so independently real, however, that Sidney became self-conscious about the implications of his writing: the circumscribed comic world of the Old Arcadia could not be accommodated in a world in which death also dwelt.

Had Sidney returned from the wars, he might never have picked up his pen again—or then, he might have: coinciding with the defeat of the Spanish Armada was the beginning of that amazing decade of output which marks the high water mark of the literary Renaissance in England. Had he been challenged to start to write again, his work would probably have taken a new tack; and, with his skill in producing and projecting voice, a turn to drama would have been artistically logical, even though socially impossible. Still, we hope that Sidney would have applauded the work of Marlowe and Shakespeare in the public theaters; for surely he would have recognized the extent to which their achievements excelled the native drama which had so embarrassed him in the Defence.

Even though Sidney did not survive to witness the great outpouring in the 1590s, his works were an integral and stimulating part of it. (Ironically, it was only because he was not alive that his works figured in this renaissance, for, because of his status, he might never have authorized their publication.) His New Arcadia, published in 1590 and reprinted in 1593 with the last three books of the Old Arcadia, together with the two editions of The Fairie Queene (1590 and 1596), made the English proud of their vernacular, which had proved at last capable of sustaining the heroic. In 1591, the publication of Astrophel and Stella taught a whole generation how to contain the rhythms of speech within the patterns of meter, thereby creating poems of simultaneous song and substance. And, The Defence of Poesie, issued three times in 1595, provided poets and dramatists—at least Shakespeare—with the theoretical basis upon which to build more sophisticated structures. In fact, such were the impact of Sidney on his age and the demand for his works that, when the Countess of Pembroke reprinted her

1593 version of the *Arcadia* in the handsome folio of 1598, she included, along with the *Defence* of 1595, versions of *Astrophel and Stella,* the *Certaine Sonets,* and *The Lady of May* from her own manuscript sources. And Sidney's influence continued to be felt: this edition of his "collected works," *The Countesse of Pembroke's Arcadia,* was reprinted thirteen times by 1739.

Notes and References

Prologue

1. John Nichols, ed., *The Progresses and Public Processions of Queen Elizabeth* (3 vols., London, 1823), II, 312–29.

Chapter One

1. See Robert Hoopes, *Right Reason in the English Renaissance* (Harvard, 1962).
2. Garrett Mattingly, *The Armada* (Boston, 1959).
3. The transcription of this letter in Feuillerat, III, 166–67, is so awkward that I have been forced to modernize it for the sake of clarity.
4. Quoted by M. W. Wallace, *The Life of Sir Philip Sidney* (London, 1915), p. 390.
5. Quoted by Wallace, p. 399.
6. George Whetstone. *Sir Philip Sidney, his honorable life, his valiant death, and true vertues* (London, 1587), sig. B2v.

Chapter Two

1. George Puttenham, *The Arte of English Poesie*, ed. by Gladys D. Willcock and Alice Walker (Cambridge University Press, 1936), p. 5, and Thomas Wilson, *The Arte of Rhetorike* (London, 1553, 1580), p. 1. All further citations in this chapter from Wilson will be noted in the text.
2. My division of the *Defence* departs from Kenneth Myrick's in *Sir Philip Sidney as a Literary Craftsman* (Harvard, 1935) mainly with regard to the *Narratio*.
3. See also Madeleine Doran, *Endeavors of Art* (Madison, Wis., 1954).
4. I have used the Latin form *Mimesis* from the *Apologie* instead of the Greek and have changed the punctuation, both for clarity.

5. Again, here and below, I have used a Latin form instead of the Greek.

6. See C. S. Lewis, *English Literature in the Sixteenth Century* (Oxford, 1954), p. 346.

7. George Gascoigne, "Certayne Notes of Instruction," *The Posies of George Gascoigne* (London, 1575), p. 291.

Chapter Three

1. See Marvin T. Herrick, "Italian Farce," *Italian Comedy in the Renaissance* (University of Illinois Press, 1960), pp. 26–59.

2. The Helmingham Hall manuscript (Hm), owned by Arthur Houghton. With the kind permission of Mr. Houghton, a transcription of *The Lady of May* prepared by Philip Murphy appeared in *Renaissance Drama, I (New Series)* (Evanston, 1968). Present quotations are drawn from that transcription.

3. Stephen Orgel, *The Jonsonian Masque* (Harvard, 1965), pp. 44–56.

4. Although this epistle was first printed in 1590 with the *New Arcadia*, with the discovery in this century of the *Old Arcadia*, scholars all agree that Sidney's remarks clearly preface the *Old* rather than the *New*.

Chapter Four

1. Roger Ascham, *The Scholemaster* (London, 1570), p. 60.

2. For a full discussion and listing, see Howard Baker, *Induction to Tragedy* (Louisiana State University Press, 1939).

3. Richard Stanyhurst, *The First Foure Bookes of Virgil His Aeneis* (Leiden, 1582), sig. A4v.

4. *Two Other very commendable Letters* (London, 1580), in *The Poetical Works of Edmund Spenser,* ed. J. C. Smith and E. De Selincourt (Oxford, 1912, 1948), p. 635.

5. Ascham, *ibid.*

6. Samuel Daniel, *A Defence of Ryme* (London, 1603), in *Samuel Daniel: Poems and A Defence of Ryme,* ed. Arthur Colby Sprague (Harvard, 1930), pp. 129, 131, 132.

7. William Empson, *Seven Types of Ambiguity* (3rd edition, London, 1953), pp. 34–36.

Chapter Five

1. In line nine, I have changed Ringler's terminal comma to a period.

2. For those who desire further argument see Buxton, and J. W. Lever, *The Elizabethan Sonnet* (London, 1956). Especially perceptive is Lever's remark: "For each poet of the Renaissance, the power to be himself had been delegated: each one imitated in order to be original" (56).

3. In line fourteen, I have not accepted Ringler's addition of quotation marks around "But ah." For support, see the review of Ringler by Jack C. Stillinger, *Journal of English and Germanic Philosophy*, LXII (April, 1963), 373–74.

4. For a possible deathbed allusion by Sidney to Lady Rich, reported in 1614, but not connecting Penelope with Stella, see Jean Robertson, "Sir Philip Sidney and Lady Penelope Rich," *Review of English Studies*, XV (August, 1964), 296–97.

Chapter Six

1. For a full account of the tradition which begins in art only in the seventeenth century, see Erwin Panofsky, "Et in Arcadia ego," *Philosophy and History: Essays presented to Ernst Cassirer*, ed. Raymond Klibansky and H. J. Paton (Oxford, 1936), pp. 223–54.

2. Ringler, p. 241. This elegy was not included in the 1590 *New Arcadia*, but a space was left for it. Although it was included by the Countess of Pembroke in the 1593 *Arcadia*, the assumption is that the poem is by her brother.

3. Transcribed by Ringler, p. 530.

Selected Bibliography

WORKS

The Prose Works of Sir Philip Sidney. Edited by Albert Feuillerat. 4 vols. Cambridge, England: Cambridge University Press, 1962. (Originally included in *The Complete Works,* 4 vols. Cambridge: Cambridge University Press, 1912–1926.) Complete prose, including the defenses of his father and Leicester and the translation of Mornay, as well as selected letters.

The Correspondence of Sir Philip Sidney and Hubert Languet. Edited by Stewart A. Pears. London: W. Pickering, 1845. Translated from Latin, this major collection of correspondence reveals Sidney's good humor and play of mind at first hand.

The Poems of Sir Philip Sidney. Edited by William A. Ringler, Jr. Oxford: Clarendon Press, 1962. Major critical edition with full introduction, notes, annotation, and bibliographies.

Sir Philip Sidney: Selected Prose and Poetry. Edited by Robert Kimbrough. Rinehart Edition 137. New York: Holt, Rinehart and Winston, 1969. Fullest one-volume edition of Sidney's works.

SECONDARY SOURCES

BOAS, F. S. *Sir Philip Sidney: Representative Elizabethan.* London: Staples Press, 1955. Sound, but not searching, "life and works" study.

BUXTON, JOHN. *Sir Philip Sidney and the English Renaissance.* London: Macmillan and Co., 1954, 1964. Excellent on the formal nature of Renaissance art and the courtly qualities of the *New Arcadia.* Perhaps overstates the roles of the Sidneys as patrons responsible for the high Renaissance in Elizabethan England.

CASTLEY, J. P., S. J. "*Astrophel and Stella*—'High Sidnaean Love' or Courtly Compliment?" *Melbourne Critical Review,* 1962 (V), 54–65. (Now *The Critical Review.*) Excellent discussion and analysis of the sequence as lyric poetry.

153

DANBY, JOHN F. "Sidney's *Arcadia*: the Great House Romance." *Poets on Fortune's Hill: Studies in Sidney, Shakespeare, Beaumont, & Fletcher.* London: Faber and Faber, 1952. Excellent study of the aristocratic basis, heroic bias, and courtly ethos of the *Arcadia*. Especially perceptive concerning the questions of sexual identity and maturity.

DAVIS, WALTER R. *A Map of Arcadia: Sidney's Romance in Its Tradition.* In *Sidney's Arcadia.* Yale Studies in English, 158. New Haven: Yale University Press, 1965. A study of the 1593 *Arcadia* as a fulfillment of Sidney's desire to write a pastoral romance. Although this thesis is not persuasive, excellent on the heritage of the *Arcadias* and on Sidney's general themes.

DORAN, MADELEINE. *Endeavors of Art: A study of form in Elizabethan drama.* Madison, Wisconsin: University of Wisconsin Press, 1954. Although primarily devoted to drama, invaluable on Renaissance literary art in general and on the *Defence* in particular.

GOLDMAN, MARCUS S. *Sir Philip Sidney and the Arcadia.* Illinois Studies in Language and Literature, XVII. Urbana: University of Illinois Press, 1934. A study of chivalric and romance values.

GREVILLE, SIR FULKE (LORD BROOKE). *The Life of the Renowned Sir Philip Sidney.* Ed. Nowell Smith. Oxford: Clarendon Press, 1907. Written ca. 1612 and published 1652, twenty-four years after Greville's death, this major biography by a lifelong friend treats his art as a reflection of Sidney's overall ideas and ideals.

HUNTER, G. K. *John Lyly: the Humanist as Courtier.* Cambridge, Mass.: Harvard University Press, 1962. Introductory chapters on sixteenth-century education and life at court provide excellent pictures of the environment in which Sidney grew.

KALSTONE, DAVID. *Sidney's Poetry: Contexts and Interpretations.* Cambridge, Mass.: Harvard University Press, 1965. Excellent on the literary traditions of "Arcadia," and on the Petrarchan heritage of *Astrophel and Stella.*

KIMBROUGH, ROBERT and PHILIP MURPHY. "The Helmingham Hall Manuscript of Sidney's *The Lady of May:* A Commentary and Transcription." *Renaissance Drama 1* (New Series). Evanston, Ill.: Northwestern University Press, 1968.

LANHAM, RICHARD A. *The Old Arcadia.* In *Sidney's Arcadia.* Yale Studies in English, 158. New Haven: Yale University Press, 1965. Good on the pastoral tradition, on the wholeness and humor, and on the "rhetorical" nature of the *Old Arcadia.*

LEWIS, C. S. "Sidney and Spenser." *English Literature in the Sixteenth Century.* Oxford: Clarendon Press, 1954. Most sound and perceptive part of a controversial book.

MOFFET, THOMAS. *Nobilis, or A View of the Life and Death of a Sidney.* Ed. and trans. Virgil B. Heltzel and Hoyt H. Hudson. San Marino, Calif.: Huntington Library, 1940. Fine example of a Renaissance moralized biography, written probably in 1593.

MONTGOMERY, ROBERT L., JR. *Symmetry and Sense: The Poetry of Sir Philip Sidney.* Austin, Texas: University of Texas Press, 1961. Excellent discussion of Sidney's development as a poet within the traditions of sixteenth-century rhetorical-poetical theory and practice.

MUIR, KENNETH. *Sir Philip Sidney.* Writers and Their Work, 120. London: Longmanz, Green, 1960. Short but perceptive introduction to Sidney (with a selected bibliography).

MYRICK, KENNETH O. *Sir Philip Sidney as a Literary Craftsman.* Cambridge, Mass.: Harvard University Press, 1935. Based on the double thesis that, while Sidney's literary ethos reflects the *sprezzatura* of Castiglione's courtier, his actual literary practice is that of the well-trained Renaissance artist. A classic of Sidney scholarship and criticism, with more emphasis on the prose than poetry.

RATHMELL, J. C. A., ed. *The Psalms of Sir Philip Sidney and The Countess of Pembroke.* Anchor Book, 311. New York: Doubleday and Co., 1963. Full introduction to, and bibliography of, the "Sydnean Psalmes." Rathmell has higher praise for the sister's work than for Sidney's.

ROSE, MARK. "Sidney's Womanish Man," *Review of English Studies,* XV (November, 1964), 353-63. Sidney "intended his readers to find Pyrocles's disguise offensive."

SPENCER, THEODORE. "The Poetry of Sir Philip Sidney," *ELH, XII* (December, 1945), 251-78. Slightly dated by its "new critical" orientation, this first full-dress study of all of the poetry *"as poetry,"* was important in drawing critical attention to Sidney and is still a valuable, sensitive study.

SPINGARN, JOEL ELIAS. *A History of Literary Criticism in the Renaissance.* New York: Columbia University Press, 1899. Sees the *Defence* only as "a veritable epitome of the literary criticism of the Italian Renaissance."

STILLINGER, JACK C. "The Biographical Problem of *Astrophel and Stella,*" *Journal of English and Germanic Philology,* LIX (October, 1960), 617-39. Patient and exhaustive examination of all of the "evidence" that Penelope was Stella. Level-headed and skeptical in its conclusions.

TANNENBAUM, S. A. *Sir Philip Sidney: A Concise Bibliography.* New York: Samuel Aaron Tannenbaum, 1941.

THOMPSON, JOHN. *The Founding of English Metre.* New York: Columbia University Press, 1961. Best book on sixteenth-century prosody ever written. Demonstrates that "Sidney discovered how to maintain a maximum tension between the language of the poem and the abstract pattern of the metre."

TILLYARD, E. M. W. *The English Epic and its Background.* New York: Oxford University Press, 1954, 1966. Contains an excellent criticism of the fragmentary *New Arcadia* as an epic, as defined by its age. Rejects the *Arcadia* of 1593 as false to Sidney's intentions.

VAN DORSTEN, J. A. *Poets, Patrons, and Professors: Sir Philip Sidney, Daniel Rogers, and the Leiden Humanists.* Leiden: Published for the Sir Thomas Browne Institute at the University Press, 1962. Especially valuable for reminding us how small and overlapping were the international literary and political worlds in the Renaissance.

WALLACE, MALCOLM WILLIAM. *The Life of Sir Philip Sidney.* Cambridge, England: Cambridge University Press, 1915. Full and detailed biography. Most neutral in its point of view. Well documented, but all sources not fully indicated.

WILES, A. G. D. "Parallel Analysis of the Two Versions of Sidney's *Arcadia,*" *Studies in Philology,* XXXIX (April, 1942), 167–206. Valuable for its summaries of the two stories in parallel columns.

WILSON, MONA. *Sir Philip Sidney.* London: Gerald Duckworth and Co., 1931. Biography; romantic in bias; sound in documentation.

WOLFF, S. L. *The Greek Romances in Elizabethan Prose Fiction.* New York: Columbia University Press, 1912. Contains a pioneering study of the sources.

YOUNG, RICHARD B. *English Petrarke: A Study of Sidney's Astrophel and Stella.* In *Three Studies in the Renaissance.* Yale Studies in English, 138. New Haven: Yale University Press, 1958. Fine study; emphasizes sonnet convention.

ZANDVOORT, R. W. *Sidney's Arcadia: A Comparison Between the Two Versions.* Amsterdam: Swets & Zeitlinger, 1929. Pioneer, detailed work of scholarship, showing Sidney's "growth."

Index

Alençon, Duke of, 24, 30
Anjou, first Duke of, see Henry III
Anjou, second Duke of, see Alençon
Ann, Princess (daughter of Edward IV), 24
Aquinas, Thomas, 33, 54
Ariasto, 25, 61
Arnold, Matthew, 99
Ascham, Roger, 19, 22, 25, 41, 59, 91, 98
Ashton, Thomas, 22
Aristotle, 40, 42, 46, 49, 50, 52, 54

Bacon, Sir Francis, 142
Baldwin, T. W., 22
Barclay, Alexander, 90
Bible, The, 95
Bishop, Morris, Petrarch And His World, 112
Boas, F. S., 153
Bodley, Thomas, 23
Breton, Nicholas, 57
Bryskett, Lodowick, 25, 122
Burghley, Lord (Sir William Cecil), 21, 25, 31
Buxton, John, 25, 38, 153

Cambridge, University of, 21, 22, 59
Camden, William, 23, 36
Campion, Edmund, 23
Campion, Thomas, 98, 99, 100, 122
Casimir, Prince, 27, 28, 29, 31
Castelvetro, 61
Castiglione, Baldassare, 43, 120
Castley, J. P., 153
Caxton, William, 90
Cecil, Anne, 21
Cecil, Sir Thomas, 32
Cecil, Sir William, see Burghley

Charles IX, 24
Chaucer, Geoffrey, 90, 91, 98, 105; Troilus And Criseyde, 57; Sir Thopas, 131
Cheke, John, 19, 22, 59, 98
Churchyard, Thomas, 57
Cicero, 92
Coleridge, Samuel Taylor, 53
Colet, John, 98
Cromwell, Thomas, 121

Danby, John F., 135, 154
Daniel, Samuel, 98; Defence of Rhyme, 99
Dante, 25, 91; Vita Nuova, 112; La Commedia, 112
Davis, Walter R., 69, 134, 143, 154
de Coligny, Admiral, 24, 25
de Coligny, Louise, Princess of Orange, 25
de L'Ecluse, Charles, 25
de Medici, Catherine, 24
Devereux, Lady Penelope, Lady Rich, Countess of Devonshire, 23, 27, 121, 122, 123
Devereux, Walter, see first Earl of Essex
Donatus, 71
Donne, John, 95
Doran, Madeleine, 22, 154
Drake, Sir Francis, 32, 36
Drant, Thomas, 39, 60, 100
Drayton, Michael, Poly Albion, 93
Dryden, John, 90, 99
Du Bellay, 113
Dudley, Catherine, see Countess of Huntington
Dudley, Guilford, 20
Dudley, Mary, see Lady Sidney

159